Roland Barthes

T0345512

Titles in the series *Critical Lives* present the work of leading cultural figures of the modern period. Each book explores the life of the artist, writer, philosopher or architect in question and relates it to their major works.

In the same series

Roland Barthes

Andy Stafford

REAKTION BOOKS

For George Stanley Baverstock (1915–)

Published by Reaktion Books Ltd
Unit 32, Waterside
44–48, Wharf Road
London N1 7UX, UK

www.reaktionbooks.co.uk

First published 2015
Copyright © Andy Stafford 2015

Printed and bound in Great Britain by Bell & Bain, Glasgow

A catalogue record for this book is available from the British Library

ISBN 978 1 78023 495 3

Contents

Notes on the Text

Quotations from Barthes' writings are taken from the published English translations. Any other translations of Barthes' work are my own and referenced to the French versions as they appear either in the five-volume *Oeuvres completes*, ed. Éric Marty (Paris, 2002) and signalled by *oc*, followed by the volume number in Roman and the page numbers in Arabic numerals, or in the posthumous volumes that have been published since 2002. All translations from other writers' work in French are mine, unless stated otherwise.

Introduction

We all have two lives: the real one, the one we have dreamed of in our childhood and which we continue to dream of as adults, through the mist; and the false one, the one we live in our relations to others, which is the practical, useful one, the one where we end up being put into a coffin.

Fernando Pessoa, *The Book of Disquiet*

If we look at the entries for various writers in the impressive *New Oxford Companion to Literature in French*, edited by Peter France (1995), we find that each and every one has a fixed and recognizable literary identity: Albert Camus – novelist, playwright, essayist; Jean-Paul Sartre – best known as a philosopher, but also novelist, dramatist, critic, moralist and so on. In contrast, Roland Barthes' entry begins 'a writer who evades classification'. Yet classification was integral to Barthes. He was an inveterate writer of lists: in index cards, in teaching notes, in many of his publications, in correspondence even. For Barthes, it was the key idea of 'combinations', cutting a sharp line across 'classification', that counted; the 'combination', although nothing but a reuse, a repackage, was key to the multifarious, potentially infinite, ways of considering an existing phenomenon.

Barthes was famously suspicious of the writer's diary or notebook. He never wrote a writer's journal, or barely did. The four texts that we might call 'journals' (his essays describing experiences in Morocco and Paris in *Incidents*, his description of his visit to China in 1974 and his *Journal de deuil* (*Mourning Diary*), written following the death of his mother) were all, rather starkly, published posthumously – that is, very possibly against his will.[1] However, much of the material in the recently published seminar of 1973–4, *Le Lexique de l'auteur* (The Author's Lexicon, Paris, 2009) – which was 'fictionalized' into *Roland Barthes by Roland Barthes* in 1975 – inaugurated a use of teaching and lecturing that inscribes the Self, his self, into the analysis, and which continues across the seminar and lecture notes that follow: the seminars on the *Discours amoureux* (A Lover's Discourse) and the lectures at the Collège de France, *Comment vivre ensemble* (How to Live Together), *Le Neutre* (The Neutral) and *La Préparation du roman* (The Preparation of the Novel), given between 1976 and 1980 (and published posthumously in French between 2002 and 2007). These notes, destined for an academic audience, all seemed to act as Barthes' 'journal', complementing the essays and books that he published in the last period of his life and which also inscribed his self into the writing.[2] Indeed, these 'new' writings, emerging from the teaching and lecturing in the last decade of Barthes' life (and his most successful commercially), seemed to gesture towards a new object, what Barthes called the *livre-cours* – the book or essay that emerges from teaching in a lecture or seminar situation.

Though not all of his teaching and lecture notes were imagined or envisaged by him as a future, published 'book', Barthes was nevertheless very aware that, if the Self became part of a teaching and research context, there was a literary production that could emerge and which could place the Self (not necessarily Barthes' self) at the centre of the reflections. Thus Barthes' work in the 1970s has opened up a more recent trend in what we might call 'auto-fiction', which, from the 1980s onwards, has undermined and redefined the biographical and autobiographical genres. In his work, however, this 'Self' is invested with a Barthesian institutional inflection: education as a place to play (out)/work (out) the Self.

As the French *nouveau romancier* Alain Robbe-Grillet put it in 1977, at the Colloque de Cerisy conference devoted to Barthes, 'I am a novelist of the '60s and '70s; you are a novelist of the future.'[3]

Barthes seems to have catered well for the future. Though he considered it a 'non-sense', Barthes' posthumous life could be seen as controlled by the skill of his writing style. In a review of Marie Gil's recent biography of Barthes, Jean-Louis Jeannelle asks whether one can really 'write a "Barthesian" biography of Barthes without pastiching him', and believes that Barthes pre-empted this option:

> Barthes deploys such a reflexive consciousness of his own analyses that his commentators risk imitating it without being able to claim to overtake or identify in him any levels of meaning that he might not have anticipated.[4]

Instead, suggests Gil, we should read Barthes with his family structures in our minds. Her example is the title of Barthes' curious reading of Honoré de Balzac's story 'Sarrasine', published as the essay *s/z* in 1970. The title ostensibly refers to the first letters of the names Sarrasine and Zambinella, the latter being the object of the former's amorous attentions in the Balzac tale. Gil relates this, in the life of Barthes, to the final letter of his own name and the middle letter of Barthes' younger half-brother, Michel Salzedo, towards whom Barthes might have held complex and conflicting feelings due to his strong attachment to their mother:

> If I identify . . . a cryptogram of 'Life' in *s/z* (the 'narrative' of his brother's birth), what interests me is not to 'read' into this the manifestation of an interior life, of the psychic repercussions on the subject, Barthes, caused by this birth (jealousy, Oedipus, etc.), and even less to explain the text by his life. Not at all; what is fascinating is to find the writing, the tracing, of a life in a text – that is, the inscription [*graphie*] of his

brother Salzedo's birth in the text *s/z*. This is where *bio-graphie* is found. This is the place in life – 'in (the) place of life' – that I am describing, and this place is an inscription [*graphie*]. The text 'in (the) place of life' is that text which is in its rightful place, but it is also the text that allows us to break with the highly simplistic idea that life is made up only of the factual.[5]

Analysing and describing someone's life thus involves value judgements, which are made (in this case, at least) in the knowledge of the finality of that person's life. Not only is the *after*life 'nonsense', in the way Barthes understood it, but, importantly for Gil, other major events 'condense the first part of his existence into a stasis, a non-time which is both the reflection and the inversion of this first part'. For 'her' Barthes, it was the 1977 tragedy of his beloved mother's demise that is this major event – after all, the mother, as Barthes put it in 1971, is the person 'who removes social alienation'; and for Gil, this bereavement, which happened nearly three years prior to his own death, defines and reforms the way in which Barthes, and we, represent his life.[6] What happens if someone's life is defined, posthumously, as having been influenced the most by an event that occurs right at the very end of that life? In other words, since the major defining event of Barthes' life (his mother's death) happened late in *his* life, we may have the outline here of the case for writing Barthes' biography 'backwards' – starting with his death and climbing back up through History, against the usual flow of biography's normal 'downwards' trajectory (from cradle to grave). Indeed, the narrative analysis practised by Barthes, especially in his notorious reading of the Balzac story in *s/z* mentioned above, suggested that all narrative (including biography) was a text that is reversible – not to mention easily made into morsels, or 'quotes', and then misquoted. In fact, the implication is that anything said about 'text' can then be said of 'life'. It is a huge claim. Then again, Barthes' deeply *social* dissolution of self into literature, into the literary essay, was, as we will see, a key component of Barthes' 'critical life'.

As we range across Barthes' life, there will be, despite the comment that he was unclassifiable, a categorization of his work. But this categorization will, paradoxically, undermine individuality, or at least the concept of the individual person. If the form, content and style of Barthes' writing are notoriously difficult to assign to a genre, the spirit of his writing is its deep connectivity to society, to the Other, to readership. The French linguist Georges Mounin once suggested that Barthes was neither a linguistics expert nor a true literary critic; instead, said Mounin, he was operating a form of modern 'social psychoanalysis'.[7] Though we will qualify Barthes' indebtedness to psychoanalysis – he was highly ambivalent about its claims and practices – we will also explore the social side of his work. This involves not simply emphasizing the collective, group-oriented Barthes – as an undergraduate at the Sorbonne University in the 1930s, he set up the Groupe de théâtre antique; in the 1940s, due to illness, he had to seek treatment for tuberculosis in the most social of medical institutions, the sanatorium; in the 1950s, he was an activist in the French popular theatre movement; in the 1960s, he was exploring clothing and fashion, theorizing them as both individual expression and as social integration into mass culture; and in the early 1970s, he studied the utopian socialist Charles Fourier and the communal phalanstery, following this study with the lecture course on 'How to Live Together' in 1976. Looking at the social side of Barthes' work will also mean exploring the very act of writing, in all its material, ideological and pleasurable dimensions, in its deep relations to society, to friends and detractors – and to the social.

Despite his and our reservations about classifying a person – reservations that we will briefly explore in this volume – Roland Barthes has nonetheless gone on to be one of the most important and frequently cited twentieth-century French writers. His thoughts, methods, essays and maxims have reverberated not just across the humanities, such as in literary and visual studies, but through the social sciences and even the 'hard' sciences (medicine, maths and even binary theory). It is important to underline, in spite of this diffuse and disseminated 'Barthes', whose ideas seem to float in the cultural wind of the *zeitgeist*, that there is an essential, sedimented 'Barthes' – that is, the Writer. However, this term needs to be tightly defined (at least in Barthes' case). Neither the 'romantic'-inspired genius, nor the plaything of surrealistic automatism, the Barthesian writer navigated a tight course between these two opposing options. Barthes achieved this by an evacuation, or bracketing, of (his) subjectivity, in which writing operated the writer's hand, rather than the other way round. The Mexican poet Octavio Paz summarizes well the consequent 'displacement of self' in the act of writing: '[W]ho drives the pen?. . ./ Someone in me is writing, moves my hand.'[8] And similar to Paz, who does not have 'the mania of the personal voice', Barthes too believed instead 'in the coherent work, composed of many voices' (to further quote Paz's prose poem).

All of Barthes' writing then attests to a gregariousness of spirit, a sociality of writing, especially in his double notion of 'thinking through others' and of others 'thinking through him'. In foregrounding the act and conditions of writing, Barthes developed not so much a cult of writing, but a practice and a salvation *through* writing. Posthumous life is a 'non-sense', but writing – as permanent trace over performance of the essay by the living writer – can still give a writer presence in his future (that is, posthumous) absence. The solitary hour, of which Paz writes, was for Barthes the morning, at home, writing between 7 am and 1 pm.

There is another dimension to this decentred writing self for Barthes, and that is the psychoanalytical category of the self outside of oneself. In an early essay from 1942, Barthes quotes, from memory, Paul Valéry's claim to have become a poet in order 'to be able to afford an exact account of the procedures of poetics'.[9]

Already in 1942, Barthes was sufficiently alert to the self-referential nature of all writing that Valéry's phrase could just as easily be attributed to Barthes. Barthes became an essayist in order 'to be able to afford an exact account of the procedures of (literary) essay-istics', hence the third person in Paz's poem, but also in Barthes' own biography of 'his self' (as opposed to an autobiography, of *himself*) in his book *Roland Barthes by Roland Barthes* of 1975.

This is not to say that Barthes held no purpose beyond the conceptualist question of 'why (and how) do I write?' It is important when reading Barthes to bear in mind that he often *suggests* something (that *is* happening, *has* been done, *could* happen), but what he really means is 'I am going to' ('I should', 'I could', 'I can' and so on). This was his 'scientific' way of doing things; it is, essentially, a strategy of rhetoric – for example, Barthes' seminal essay 'The Death of the Author' of 1967 announced the birth of the writer, but perhaps it was as *his* birth as a writer, as *his* radical move into what he called *écriture* (writing). Thus the implication that the 'scriptor' is already in the mind of the reader represents a good example of a decentring of self, a (re-)socialization of subjectivity.[10]

This undermining of the traditional, 'normal', individual self was then part of what Barthes called – in his trademark use of ancient Greek terms – *maché*. Far from the Self being consistent, Barthes (following André Gide) wanted to show how we oscillate, how we do not have a synthesis of the contradictions within each of our lives, in what Barthes called an 'open dialectic', because this Self is plural, multiple and social.[11]

Roland Barthes at home, 1975.

1

War Orphan

Born on 12 November 1915 into a middle-class but financially modest family in Cherbourg, on the tip of Northern France, Roland Gérard Barthes and his family were beset with tragedy before his first birthday. On 27 October 1916 his father Louis Barthes, commander of the auxiliary patrol boat the *Montaigne* – a rapidly converted trawler built in Great Yarmouth in 1912 and commissioned by the French navy between 1914 and 1919 – was hit by enemy fire on his very first patrol. His ship was sunk after an attack from five German torpedo boats in the English Channel at Cap Gris-Nez (between Boulogne and Calais). *Commandant* and *enseigne de vaisseau de première classe auxiliaire* (sub-lieutenant) Louis Barthes was posthumously cited by the French navy and made a *Chevalier de la Légion d'honneur*. His father's death on the *Montaigne* is the first of three ironies in Roland Barthes' life, which complement the three paradoxes in his work identified by Patrizia Lombardo.[1] The great French essayist Michel de Montaigne (whose name will return, in uncanny fashion, in Chapter Two, when we encounter Barthes' secondary school in Paris) was not only the major influence on the style of writing that Barthes would go on to produce (the essay), but the name of the ship that made Barthes into a war orphan. From that early paternal bereavement onwards, Barthes' personal and family life – living with his mother all of his life and his complex relationship with his younger half-brother could, arguably, be explained, if only in part, by the *Montaigne* disaster.

The second important family irony, for a theorist who has been regularly mobilized by postcolonial criticism in recent years in order to expose colonial ideology, is that Barthes' maternal grandfather Louis Binger was a military explorer whose name was given, on its 'discovery' by French forces, to the port of Bingerville in the Ivory Coast in West Africa, a French colony at the time, of which Binger became colonial governor. Author of *Du Niger au golfe de Guinée par le pays Kong et le Mossi* (From Niger to the Gulf of Guinea via the Lands of the Kong and the Mossi, 1892), Louis Binger was a gifted linguist, historian, anthropologist and cartographer, who published his memoirs in 1936. During the inauguration of the Eiffel Tower in Paris in 1889, Binger met Noémi Lepet, who he subsequently married. Their second child, Henriette, Roland Barthes' mother, was born in 1893 – neither of Binger's children is mentioned in the memoirs of 1936, possibly because he and Noémi were divorced in 1900. Noémi went on to remarry, this time to Louis Révelin, a Socialist Party leader and friend of the pacifist politician and Great War opponent Jean Jaurès.

Barthes' paternal grandfather's family could not have been more different. Whereas the Binger family was from Alsace, in eastern, predominantly Protestant France, the Barthes family was distinctly southwest in origin. Catholic, with impoverished lawyers by background on his paternal grandfather's side, but from a wealthy set of nobles of the region on his paternal grandmother's, Léon Barthes, Barthes' grandfather, had been a lowly state employee in France's southern railways; consequently, the Barthes family had been unable to support Louis, Barthes' father, through university, and in 1903 he had to join the navy. Thus when he and Barthes' mother, Henriette, herself career-less and barely recognized by her explorer father, met, married and started a family, theirs was an impoverished household.

Once orphaned in 1916, Barthes moved with his mother to live with her in-laws, his paternal grandparents, in Bayonne, a provincial town of 27,000 inhabitants in southwest France and the regional capital of the Basque country. Here Barthes had his earliest memories and went to primary school in the inner suburb of Marracq, thus beginning a lifelong attachment to the Basque region where Barthes is now buried in a grave next to his mother. Indeed, despite being born at the other end of the country (in Cherbourg, Normandy), by growing up in Bayonne Barthes became attached to the region to such an extent that he saw himself as 'coming' from the southwest, although never claiming to be Basque. By 'being' or becoming the writer from the southwest, Barthes was merely illustrating a general point: one's early childhood and adolescence are marked by experiences based on geographical and local character. Though Bayonne was part only of Barthes' early adolescence (he had moved to Paris by the age of ten), he had enough memories to see the southwest as a spiritual home. In his later career, when he began to theorize the voluntary memory work of the adult brain, in his notion of voluntary 'anamnesis' (unforgetting), he used the smells and tastes of Bayonne that he encountered between 1915 and 1924, in highly Proustian fashion, to think through the impact of childhood experience on the adult, suggesting that the older and more distant from these early experiences we are, the more we rely on memory triggers and associations to conjure them up.

As a young infant, before reaching primary school age, Barthes was looked after during the day by a young, local Basque woman, Marie Latxague, allowing him to play with the middle-class children nearby. Barthes' class position as a child – impoverished but middle class – had a particular effect on his upbringing and identity. He recounted in a radio interview in 1975 that he lived a loved but isolated existence as a child alone with his mother, since the only visits he made were to see his grandparents during the holidays.[2] Brought up by his mother, in difficult circumstances, Barthes nevertheless benefited from the presence and affection of two formidable older women: his 'Tante' Alice, a professional piano teacher, who taught him piano (mainly Schumann, and then Ravel and Bach), and Berthe Barthes, who was Léon Barthes' widow and Roland Barthes' paternal grandmother. 'My family was essentially a feminine family', but, with no other male family member, it was also a 'family without familialism'.[3] *Ennui* (boredom) would be a key word for the middle-aged Barthes of the 1960s and '70s. But living during his formative years in the quiet and relaxed region of the Basque country meant that, geographically, Barthes was like many French writers and thinkers brought up in the provinces but forever marked by their northern roots (Gide, Sartre, Foucault). For Barthes' recent biographer Marie Gil, this dualism, or two sides, becomes Bayonne and Paris, two different worlds, whose differences were seen by Barthes in 1975 as 'corporeal': Paris equalled 'alert, tired', and the southwest 'rested, heavy'.[4]

In this safe but rather boring upbringing, Barthes developed interests in reading and music and explored, often alone, the quieter streets of provincial Bayonne. Bayonne had become a distinctly bourgeois town following the rise of the steel and coal industries supplying the railways, but after the First World War, its port had fallen into decline. Similarly, Barthes' southwest family had fallen into economic decline, despite being bourgeois by culture and heritage. It is not surprising then that social class – including any possibility of escaping the class identity one is forced to take on – was to become a key theme in Barthes' writing thirty years later. That he and his mother had to wait until 1925 for him to be officially 'adopted by the State' as a war orphan and for his mother to receive a war pension was another factor in the family's impoverishment.

That we have linked the *Montaigne* – the death of the father – to Barthes' career as essayist in the great French Montaigne tradition has its echo in the recent biography by Gil, analysing Barthes' (third-person) commentary on his own psychic make-up, especially what he called the 'matrix' in relation to his father's absence. 'The death of the father and writing in fragments seem linked', according to Gil, who points to the etymology of the name 'Barthes' as 'hole', the hole was the emptiness in which Barthes had been left as a young boy by an entirely absent and absented father.[5] This 'hole' that Barthes seemed to have been in extended to his social class, as he put it in 1970: 'a quarter landowning bourgeoisie a quarter for mer nobility, two quarters liberal bourgeoisie, all rubbed up together and united by a general impoverishment'.[6] As we have seen, although the Barthes family came from a bourgeois, educated background, and despite having a rich and well-connected maternal grandmother in the form of Noémi Révelin – ex-wife of colonial explorer Louis Binger and wife of wealthy Socialist Party philosophy teacher and politician Louis Révelin – they did not have much money in Barthes' early years. It is perhaps easy to underestimate the importance of this (slightly distant) family connection for Roland Barthes. If only in financial terms, Noémi was to play a key role when she died in 1953, as her daughter, Barthes' mother, was able to inherit a good sum of money (including a car and a house in Hendaye). Furthermore, her husband – Barthes' step-grandfather – knew the poet Paul Valéry, the famous anti-war politician Jean Jaurès and all those linked to the left-leaning journal of the first fifteen years of the twentieth century, the *Cahiers de la quinzaine*. (Founded by Charles Péguy, the *Cahiers* had been an important defender of the Jewish French army artillery officer Alfred Dreyfus, who was falsely convicted, during a wave of anti-Semitism in France, of passing secrets to the Prussians).

Between 1916 and 1924, regular annual family visits in the summer to stay with Noémi in Paris encouraged Barthes' mother Henriette to move nearer to her mother. Thus in 1924 she and Roland found modest accommodation in Saint-Germain-des-Prés, a quartier in central Paris where Barthes would live for the rest of his life. This is not to say that the southwest, the Basque country of his childhood, did not mark and remain with him. Indeed, as we have already suggested, the 'Paris versus Basque country' double-sided-ness to Barthes is merely part of the 'oscillation' in his personality. The other area in which Barthes might have been beholden to a dualism was his Protestant upbringing in a deeply Catholic country, again not unlike his literary forbear and hero André Gide, who was raised in an austere Protestant family but always tempted throughout his life to convert to Catholicism. With his (Catholic) father dead, Barthes was brought up in his mother's Calvinist faith. As a young man, Barthes even toyed with the idea of becoming a pastor, and he regularly attended the Oratoire du Louvre, a Protestant church with liberal leanings in central Paris, between the years 1930 and 1934.

It is important to stress that the move to Paris, the leaving behind of the southwest, was partly a financial decision. Henriette – Barthes' mother – had very little training or skill with which to supplement her meagre war pension. Bookbinding in Paris became her main source of income while Barthes began junior school. Remembering not having had enough money to eat anything more than bread and pâté for a few days, he insisted in later life that this poverty was social (panic over the cost of a school uniform, shoes, school books and even food), rather than cultural; thus he would later stress that, of the two great determinants in life – one's material conditions and then one's sexual impulses – it was the former that troubled him in his adolescent life. Indeed, there is a stark contradiction in his class identity. Though Barthes never felt that he was part of middle-class society in financial and societal terms, he benefited nevertheless from the trappings of a middle-class upbringing: a piano, books and intellectual connections in the family. In fact, it was not so much poverty that the Barthes family experienced in the 1920s and '30s, but, as he later declares, hardship.

Finally being officially accepted as a *pupille de la nation* (war orphan) soon after his tenth birthday in November 1925 no doubt helped his struggling mother, who had to trundle off every day from Saint-Germain-des-Prés in central Paris to Courbevoie, west of Paris, where she fulfilled the bookbinder's job for which she was not especially fitted. Montaigne came back for Barthes in another guise in this early adolescent period, from 1924 to 1930. Barthes followed in the footsteps of Jean-Paul Sartre by attending the Lycée Montaigne in Paris, where (unlike Sartre) Barthes was a model pupil with excellent potential, in spite of being left-handed at a time when this trait of one-in-ten people was (often cruelly) 'corrected'.[7] This early academic success was to be completely forestalled when Barthes became ill with tuberculosis in 1934, thus starting a long period of relapses and lengthy treatments that would mar his life until 1946 and seriously curtail any chance of establishing a career.[8]

Barthes made lifelong friends at the Lycée Montaigne, including Philippe Rebeyrol. In 1930 he and Rebeyrol went to the Lycée Louis-le-Grand for *le troisième* (Year Eleven in today's British schooling), and both did equally well, especially in literature, history and classical languages. In April 1933, while writing a first novel – said to be 'Flaubertian' in inspiration, having recently read Flaubert's *L'Éducation sentimentale* (Sentimental Education) – Barthes formed the literary group l'Abbaye de Thélème with Rebeyrol. This was meant to become the title of a literary journal that never appeared, Barthes' contribution being a version of an ancient Greek story entitled *En marge du 'Criton'* (In the Margins of *Crito*). Picking up on the vogue in the 1930s for the literary pastiche – exemplified by the series of pastiches by Jules Lemaître, which are all called *En marge de . . .* (In the Margins of . . .) – Barthes changed the ending of *Crito*, one of the dialogues attributed to Plato. In Barthes' pastiche version, Socrates eats the figs, escaping death.[9] Barthes continued his pastiches, sending another to Rebeyrol from his first 'cure' for tuberculosis in the mountains: *Le Voyage d'Arion* (The Voyage of Arion) was a brief play, following Herodotus' account, on illness and ancient Greek paganism that addressed Rebeyrol directly in the words of a man who was ill and bored.

Unsurprisingly, though always slightly behind Rebeyrol, Barthes did well in the first part of his *baccalauréat* (equivalent to British A-levels) in 1933. These results helped him, with additional family support, to secure funding for further studies. Barthes benefited from a letter from Paul Valéry in 1933 to the minister of education, which supported his application for a university grant – such were the financial difficulties for the Barthes family in Paris, but also the connections provided by Henriette's mother, Noémi.[10]

During this adolescent period, Barthes began to develop interests in cinema (Charlie Chaplin, mainly) and literature. There were many books at home – not only because his mother worked in bookbinding, but because of the family's links to the liberal bourgeoisie (via Noémi and Louis Révelin, above all) – such as works by Gide, Jules Verne, Stéphane Mallarmé and Jean Jaurès. In 1932 Marcel Proust's magnum opus, *À la recherche du temps perdu* (Remembrance of Things Past), was recommended to him by Tante Alice. This was a period when Barthes was engaged in the writing of two different novels: one, *Île joyeuse* (Joyful Island), was about a personal, pagan religion; and the other, *L'Histoire de Judith* (The Story of Judith), was a love story. But soon Barthes abandoned his ideas for a novel, thinking instead of writing an analysis of petit bourgeois ideology, an idea that would resurface in *Mythologies* twenty years later. He also read (and was inspired by) Jaurès, Anatole France and Valéry, all of which was augmented by his reading of the moderate-left, anti-clerical newspaper *L'Oeuvre*. At this time, Barthes also developed a passion for singing. He would soon become a pupil of the famed French singer Charles Panzéra (having, most probably, seen Panzéra in 1931 singing Valéry's libretto for Arthur Honegger's lyrical drama *Amphion*), and one of Barthes' first (male) loves was a fellow student singer, Michel Delacroix (son of Henri, the philosopher of language and friend of Henri Bergson). Delacroix joined Barthes in his lessons with Panzéra and was, like Barthes, a tuberculosis victim; he succumbed to the illness in 1942. It was Panzéra to whom Barthes would unfavourably compare the singer Gérard Souzay as 'bourgeois' in *Mythologies*.[11]

This distinctly social – if not affective – side to Barthes' cultural and amateur activities was further confirmed with his interest in theatre. In the early 1930s he was a regular visitor to the theatres of Charles Dullin and Georges Pitoëff – the so-called 'Cartel' theatres – especially Mathurins and L'Atelier, where Barthes was especially impressed by Dullin's acting never 'incarnating' his role. Thus, before discovering Brecht's epic theatre in the 1950s, Barthes was already sensitive to the need to 'distance' the actor from their role. Barthes was so inspired by theatre in November 1935 that, on his return from his first attempt to treat his tuberculosis in Bedous (in the Pyrenees), which had started in October 1934, he was keen to extend his enthusiasm for theatre to his student activities. This decision was almost exactly coterminous with his having renounced the idea of joining Rebeyrol in *hypokhâgne* – the prestigious *classes préparatoires* (preparatory classes) for entry into the École normale supérieure (the equivalent of the Universities of Oxford and Cambridge). Such was the extent of his illness that he declined to follow Rebeyrol into the demanding world of *hypokhâgne* and decided instead to sign up at the Sorbonne for a degree in classics. Though a disappointment, this move was an opportunity to explore his thespian interests. In 1936, with Rebeyrol (now in *hypokhâgne*) and another close friend, Jacques Veil (who was soon to die in the Second World War), Barthes set up the Groupe de théâtre antique de la Sorbonne. This group put on classical theatre in the Sorbonne courtyard for the next three years until the outbreak of war, although spending time and energy on this extracurricular activity was to the obvious detriment of Barthes' university studies.

The key experience for Barthes – other than theatre activism, set design and performance production – was that of acting and speaking his lines. The very day after the radical left-wing government in France, the Front Populaire (Popular Front), came to power on a wave of anti-fascism, the Groupe performed Aeschylus' play *The Persians*, in which Barthes played the ghost of Darius. His role was to utter words of warning to Xerxes of the dangers and vanities of war and revenge from the palace steps. Barthes would later describe the intense fear of getting his weighty words wrong, of being tempted to think of something else instead of the lines to say, but he also hinted at a certain distance between actor and character. Not only was this to become a key Brechtian motif for Barthes in the popular theatre of the 1950s, but it pointed to a central notion in Barthes' writing – namely, that there is a gap, a qualitative difference even, between the voice of a writer and the writer himself. It is not so much that language translates the writing self, rather that the writer, and the voice of writing, are distinct activities, functions and therefore values for the reader. Barthes would go on to argue, prove and show that this 'doubling', or pluralizing, of the self in writing is not restricted to fiction, but involves all forms of writing.

This period of 1936–9 was a deeply Hellenist one for Barthes, not only in terms of theatre, but in his reading and travels. In July 1938, having been to Debreczen, Hungary, as a university tutor in the summer of 1937, Barthes went with the students in the Groupe antique to visit Greece, stopping in Athens, the Peloponnese, Mycenae, Argos and the islands of Delos, Aegina and Santorini, finally returning via Italy. In good Gidian style, Barthes' account of his visit concentrated on the sensual, impressionistic experience, the resulting tone of his travel narrative sounding very much like the hedonistic Gide of his (unclassifiable) work of 1897, *Les Nourritures terrestres* (Fruits of the Earth).[12] Barthes was also reading at this time – early for 'post-war' intellectuals such as Barthes – an essay by Friedrich Nietzsche on the fundamental place of tragedy in human society; indeed, his very first publication in 1942, in the student journal *Cahiers de l'étudiant*, was a reading of Nietzsche's *The Birth of Tragedy*. Though twelve years later Barthes would go on to reject tragedy for the modern world in favour of Brecht's epic theatre, he nevertheless saw, from this early period onwards, the possibility of a truly human – not simply aesthetic – communion in the theatre, a truly social experience of showing 'the human enigma in all its essential meagreness'.[13]

Barthes also attended Paul Valéry's inaugural lecture at the Collège de France in December 1937 (nearly forty years before his own inaugural lecture at the same prestigious institution). Given that literature was usually studied as part of its history in this pre-war period, Valéry's lecture was heavily criticized for its insistence on the importance of poetics, leading to a dismissal of his thought throughout the 1950s and '60s. Indeed, Valéry's thoughts on poetics were resurrected in the late 1960s, when poetics became a key element of literary and political analysis; it is not a coincidence then that the title of one of Barthes' prose collections, *Tel Quel* (As Is), was precisely the name that would be given to the avant-garde journal with which Barthes would be staunchly associated from the mid-1960s onwards.

Meanwhile, Henriette Barthes had added half-brother Michel to Barthes' life and household in 1927, having borne the child to a married man, André Salzedo, from whom Michel would take his surname.[14] As we have noted, Barthes' recent biographer, Marie Gil, argues that the psychoanalytical effect on Barthes is not historically but textually evident in his work, most clearly in the title of his 1970 essay *s/z*: rather than the S of Sarrasine in the Balzac story confronting the Z of the desired singer Zambinella, the S of Barthes, suggests Gil, confronts, in family and Oedipal relations, the Z of Salzedo. This is a good example of the 'fictional' biography Gil has written: Barthes, she is keen to show, played out his own personal and familial alienation and angst in his writing. From this stems her view that Barthes was an 'oscillator': for every position, idea or critique that Barthes took up in his writing, we can find its opposite (its oscillated opposition) in other parts of his writing at different stages of his career. She does, however, fall short of imparting some modern mental imbalance to Barthes, such as bipolar disorder or other illness that elicits wide swings – oscillations – in one's personality. Instead, she sees Barthes as philosophically unable or unwilling to synthesize opposites, preferring to hold them in mobile tension with each other, only then to swing between them. We will see this in the way that, in the mid-1950s, Barthes advocated Alain Robbe-Grillet's narratively challenging novels for their 'literalness', while admonishing Camus for his allegorical approach to the novel in his 1947 allegory of Nazism, *La Peste* (The Plague). Yet, only ten years later in 1966 (in *Criticism and Truth*, as we shall see in Chapter Four), he would roundly reject 'old' critics' stubborn refusal to go beyond literalism, to find and explore the symbolism of literature. Similarly, being 'neutral' as a critic was bitterly exposed as a myth of objectivity in *Mythologies* in 1957, and yet in 1977, twenty years later, Barthes would vaunt the 'neutral' in his lecture series.

It is difficult not to see this 'oscillation' as, if not downright self-contradiction, then as a sign of Barthes' favoured image, that of the spiral. But in personal terms, as Gil strongly hints, it was the absence of the father that invited (allowed for) the wilful demolition of theories by their opposites. Gil uses this psychoanalytical category of paternal loss – which she sees, following Barthes, as a 'fictional' (if plausible) explanation – as a (perhaps not 'the') context in which Barthes explored numerous binary oppositions across his career. Gil's 'fictional' biography underlines the importance of Barthes' relationship with his mother throughout his life. Put simply, Gil's argument is that it was not until his mother's death in 1977 that Barthes was able to leave the (psychoanalytically defined) 'hole' that his semi-orphaned status had left him in, the Oedipally confused presence (via absence) of the father, which created the constant 'oscillation' between binaries that so marked Barthes' career. His mother's demise merely revealed the Emptiness, the psychoanalytical Lack that was finally found after 1977, she having filled that void for most of Barthes' life until then.[15]

The advantage of underlining this life structure is twofold. First, we can begin to accept and understand (and then explore) the gaping contradictions in Barthes' imagination and writing; we can see the constant refusal to synthesize as a moment of essayistic provisionality. But we can also appreciate the combative, antagonistic nature and self-consciousness of the 'positions' or 'stances' that Barthes adopted across his career, until, suggests Gil, the death of his mother. Indeed, Gil makes a key point about Barthes' life and career, given the end-loaded significance of his life, and this is the third great irony of Barthes' life: its most defining event, his mother's death, came right at its end. She suggests, following Barthes' radical reconsideration of his life, of life generally, after his mother's demise in 1977, that we have access to Barthes' biography only via this ending, that the death of the mother 'revealed' his life to him (she uses a photographic metaphor deliberately) and reorganized – albeit retrospectively – how Barthes considered his past.[16] We might object that Gil is merely using hindsight to characterize Barthes' life, but this was precisely how Barthes considered his childhood and adolescence in later life when, in his writing and lectures in the 1970s, he used his earlier life as material for his research and teaching. One could argue then, given the backwards way in which the older Barthes revisited his younger life (at the age of 60 in 1975), that he was objectifying it into a distanced, almost alien person; yet, in psychoanalytical terms, not to mention a Marxist, historical-materialist optic, family structures, origins and class experiences in one's youth are key determinants of that 'Other' who is the same person but 'different' because he is grown much older. We will see the benefit of this alienating effect of looking at his childhood from a temporal distance in the final chapters of this book.

The key point in Barthes' early career was that Marxism and psychoanalysis – representing, respectively, social and personal solutions to the conflicts of the self and/in society – entered into competition, or rather, into an unhappy marriage in his writing, neither of them able to overcome his fundamental ambivalence towards them both. This is the reason for the underlying concern in Barthes' writing with alienation and (utopian) disalienation – somewhat rudely referred to as Barthes having a *grognon* (grumpy) personality by Calvet. It is possible that humour was not an especially Barthesian trait (beyond his use of sarcasm and irony); then again, pleasure and disalienation are a serious business! It is not surprising then – and we do not need to borrow Gil's psychoanalytical framework to appreciate this – that Barthes should become interested in a mode of thought, semiology, which specifically operates in binary constructions, oscillating endlessly, inconclusively, between positions.

The other major influence on Barthes' career from the adolescent period of his life was the experience of near-death, of isolation and of a stunted academic career caused by the serious illness that started in 1934. In that same year, having formed a group of young anti-fascists, the DRAF (Défense républicaine anti-fasciste), in his school class, in order to challenge the larger group of Jeunesses patriotes – who had been sucked in by the growth of fascism – he and Rebeyrol went to the demonstration on 9 February against the *ligues fascistes*. These groups, following Hitler's Nazis in Germany, had tried to instigate a putsch against the French parliament a few days before. Fortunately, 12 February 1934 saw a huge (and, importantly, united) demonstration of communists and socialists in Paris that crushed the fascist uprising in France, and which no doubt inspired the Popular Front government that came to power in May 1936. This politicization in France was, however, cut short for

Barthes. Two months before he was due to sit the philosophy component of the *baccalauréat* exam, and ready to go with Rebeyrol into *hypokhâgne*, disaster struck: Barthes suffered a haemoptysis in the left lung, the spitting-up of blood often associated with tuberculosis. (Barthes, like Albert Camus, was a *tubard*, a person suffering from tuberculosis.) This began a long period of illness (1934–46), during which Barthes had to go through numerous consultations and clinics for a cure that eluded many of his generation. He managed to get his health back the following year but then in 1935 he had to seek treatment in the Pyrenees as a way of avoiding the (dreaded) sanatorium. His first stay was in Bedous, where he sat in bed in the quiet and had time to read works by François Mauriac, Jean Giraudoux and even Balzac.

As well as having a huge social and developmental impact on the twenty-year-old Barthes, his illness undermined his academic career.[17] It was not only his best friend, Rebeyrol, who went to *hypokhâgne* without him; another contemporary in *hypokhâgne*, who was to reappear in the joust with him over new criticism in the mid-1960s, was none other than the future Racine specialist and Sorbonne professor Raymond Picard. If we combine this stunted academic progression, fear of mortality and deep personal uncertainty about his career with the loss of his father and his exclusion, because of his illness, from the national experience of Nazi occupation and eventual liberation from tyranny (Etienne Révelin, Barthes' mother's step-brother, was killed in the Paris street-fighting of January 1945), we can see that Barthes' life was beset, directly and indirectly, with the tragedies of the first half of the twentieth century of war, bereavement and poverty.

2

Tubard

Barthes had had experience of illness already in his childhood – ear problems meant having to miss school, which gave him ample opportunity to read. Nothing prepared him for the experience of tuberculosis, however. As we have seen, it had a disastrous effect on a promising academic career. Not only did being a *tubard* exclude Barthes from the *classes préparatoires* of the *grandes écoles*, but it prevented him from completing his degree with a *diplôme d'études supérieures* (or DES, equivalent today to a research master's degree). Furthermore, as war was about to break out in 1939, he had to content himself with becoming a teacher at a school in Biarritz where his younger half-brother, Michel Salzedo, was a pupil. At the end of that year, following the Nazi invasion in 1940, he went to Paris to be a *répétiteur* teacher (student-helper for schoolchildren) at two schools, the Lycées Carnot and Voltaire. He was finally able to complete his DES on Greek tragedy in 1941, in spite of the return of his tuberculosis in October of that year.

During this period, despite the looming need to visit a sanatorium for his tuberculosis, Barthes' experience was not limited to adversity: it was at this time that he began his amorous relationship with Michel Delacroix, as they both attended classes by the singer Charles Panzéra. Later, Barthes would claim that Panzéra had as big an impact on him as did the theatre of Brecht in the 1950s: in short, Panzéra taught him how to 'work the text'. However, in 1941, just as his friend Philippe Rebeyrol received his *agrégation* (the prestigious qualification for exceptional teachers) and became a French teacher in Spain, Berthe Barthes, Barthes' paternal grandmother, died, and Barthes had a relapse in his lung. Therefore, in January 1942, Barthes had no choice but to make his first visit to the dreaded sanatorium. Here began a four-year period of regular treatment, first in Saint-Hilaire-du-Touvet in the French Alps near Grenoble, between 1942 and 1943. He returned to Paris for a 'post-cure' in the new tuberculosis centre in the rue de Quatrefages in spring 1943 (which, fortunately, allowed him to complete the last section of his degree, the *certificat* in grammar and philology), only for his right lung to suffer another relapse in July 1943, requiring another stay in Saint-Hilaire-du-Touvet until late 1944. This was followed by another 'post-cure', this time in Leysin, Switzerland, between 1945 and 1946.

So between 1942 and 1946 – the main part of the war and the liberation of France – Barthes, a young French man, 'missed' most of the action, holed up in sanatoria with limitless books as a way of passing time. Was it any wonder that his life might become as literature – Barthes often referred to his reading of *the* novel about life, *The Magic Mountain* by Thomas Mann, in a sanatorium for tuberculosis – or even that literature was his life? Furthermore, was it any wonder that he might feel, in generational terms, that he was six years younger?

Barthes had been *classé* (classified) not only as a *pupille de la nation* (as we saw in Chapter One), but as a *tubard*. The *enfermement* (imprisonment) that being a tuberculosis sufferer entailed led to a variety of forms of classification, in the social sphere (danger of social contagion, lingering air of death), but also in bodily terms. The sanatorium involved a life that was enclosed – monastic even – but never far from death; the *tubard* had to sit his time out. Late in 1975 Barthes went on to discuss this influence on the 'body'. In *Roland Barthes by Roland Barthes*, he described the pile of papers stapled at the end of the bed: 'a farcical way of writing one's body within time', the 'body' being his 'mana-word' in 1975.[1] Also, after his further relapse in 1943, Barthes had to remain lying down motionless for long periods, with his head down and legs higher than his head, in order to rest his lungs for three months, in what was called a *cure de déclive*, the other requirement being absolute silence. Not surprisingly, Barthes had even more time to read extensively. He developed, above all, a fascination for the nineteenth-century romantic historian Jules Michelet and, in particular, for the manner in which Michelet's body was inscribed into his writing of history. While reading Michelet closely, he designed his own makeshift note-taking system on a series of *fiches* (cards), which (now available for consultation in the Bibliothèque nationale in Paris) would no doubt today be the envy of any computer-designed literary archive.

It was also during his stay in Saint-Hilaire-du-Touvet in 1943 that he started to consider a career in psychiatric medicine, beginning a *certificat d'études physiques, chimiques et biologiques* (PCB), the foundational qualification for the first year of a medicine degree, though this was interrupted by his relapse. This was typical of Barthes' life – what seemed to be a total disaster in social, academic and developmental terms became its opposite: a great opportunity to explore, research and (crucially for our view of the 'social' Barthes) become part of a community.

Attached to the University of Grenoble, the sanatorium at Saint-Hilaire-du-Touvet offered plenty of classes and extra-curricular activities – all the more astounding given that these events occurred in the middle of the Second World War (and that the Vercors region around Grenoble was known for its Resistance activity against the Nazis). Barthes took full advantage of this, becoming the chronicler of the chamber music performances in the (impressive) in-house journal at Saint-Hilaire-du-Touvet, *Existences*. Thus, in a phrase attributed to Barthes, the sanatorium was a sort of 'Alpine Oxford'.[2]

Barthes found himself among some illustrious co-sufferers at Saint-Hilaire-du-Touvet, such as the philosopher François Châtelet (who was the uncle of eminent Barthes scholar and friend Éric Marty) and Joseph Baruzi, brother of the Leibniz scholar and St John of the Cross specialist Jean Baruzi. The people whom Barthes met in the sanatorium were not all beneficial to him, however. Georges Canetti (brother of the writer Elias) revealed Barthes' homosexuality to Rebeyrol, who was apparently shocked.[3] Furthermore, tragedy was never far away in the world of the *tubard*. Michel Delacroix, his first friend and lover, died of tuberculosis in 1942. Then in 1943 Barthes fell in (unrequited) love with another *tubard*, Robert David; he also struck up a friendship in the sanatorium with François Ricci, the future editor of the works of the Italian Marxist Antonio Gramsci. Thus not only was life in Saint-Hilaire-du-Touvet like an 'Alpine Oxford', it was similar to life in a phalanstery, as intricately described by the utopian socialist Charles Fourier: with rites, constraints and protections. A number of Barthes' much later projects – *Sade, Fourier, Loyola* (1971) and the 'How to Live Together' lectures (1976) – would directly reflect this experience of communal, intellectual living.

During this time, his music improved, as he practised Bach and Schumann on the piano. In charge of the well-stocked library, Barthes also developed his knowledge of literary culture rapidly in this 'Alpine Oxford', especially through his reading of poetry – Michaux, Valéry, Baudelaire and Walt Whitman in translation. These were important modernist poets on whom he gave a series of lectures at the sanatorium. Furthermore, Marie Gil attributes a lecture to Barthes under a pseudonym (Émile Ripert), in which he outlined a rejection of anarchism in poetry.[4] Other literary pieces by him were published in *Existences*: on Albert Camus' novel *L'Étranger* (The Stranger), which was to be the basis of the blank writing identified by Barthes in the 'degree zero' thesis of his first book in 1953; on the pleasure of reading the classics, which was an

A passion for playing the piano lasted all of Barthes' life.

interesting debut for the literary-critical career to come; and the piece on Gide's diary, which also contained many premonitions of his later writing career, if only on the level of the fragmentary approach adopted in it.[5] As well as Nietzsche, Barthes was beginning to explore Marxism, via the work of the American philosopher Sidney Hook, who, in his early career, had been influenced by Karl Korsch and had defended Trotsky's writing on Marxism. Barthes was also reading Marx's *Eighteenth Brumaire of Louis Bonaparte*, *The Holy Family* and *Critique of the Gotha Programme*.

However, it was literary writing that fascinated him. His article of 1942 on Gide's diaries showed a young man eager to join the ranks of writers. Later he would underline that it was his reading of Gide that had made him want to write.[6] There is another sense in which the experience of the Saint-Hilaire-du-Touvet sanatorium opened up a life of writing before him: looking back in 1976 at this period in the sanatorium – appropriately in his lecture course 'How to Live Together' – Barthes underlined the life tonic that near-death and illness can instil. Indeed, following the death of his mother in 1977, Barthes would alight on the idea of being born again, of founding a new life – what he called, following Michelet and Dante, the *vita nova*. It was not simply the copious amount of food in the sanatorium (and Barthes was known by his friends to have a voracious appetite) that could give the patients a feeling of starting life again; it was the experience of coming through the illness, while others clearly were not going to make it.

Barthes was still in Saint-Hilaire-du-Touvet when the war finished. Soon, however, thanks to financial support from Swiss banks in Berne, a number of the *tubards* – including Barthes and Robert David – were moved, in February 1945, to a sanatorium in Leysin, Switzerland, which was more in touch with the outside world, offering visits to Swiss families. Barthes was certainly not out of the woods yet: even when he was better and allowed to recuperate in Leysin, suddenly he had to undergo an operation, involving the removal of part of a rib to graft onto the lung, an unused part of which was given to him afterwards as a bizarre memento. Later Barthes would narrate chucking this body part out of the window as if for a dog to eat. The implication was that the body, like the written fragment so typical of Barthes' writing style, was something that one throws out to be consumed, and, by extension, that writing is a part of the body.[7]

While in Leysin, waiting for the treatment to be completed, Barthes befriended an important person for his later political and intellectual trajectory: Georges Fournié, a typographer by trade, was a follower of the small Trotskyist groupings trying to bring non-Stalinist Marxist politics to bear on the fight against fascism. Arrested by the Gestapo in 1943, Fournié was lucky to survive Buchenwald concentration camp, having been released with tuberculosis. Barthes met Fournié in October 1945, just after his operation at Leysin. Barthes had read Marx's *Holy Family*, and so was open to the Marxism, a specifically Trotskyist version, that Fournié discussed with him in intense debates between autumn 1945 and spring 1946. This was also the time when Sartre's existentialism was in the ascendency, with the launch of *Les Temps modernes* (Modern Times). Sartre represented Barthes' entry into modern literature – or rather modern thought, since all the works by Sartre that Barthes read during the war and just as it finished (*Being and Nothingness*, *Outline for a Theory of the Emotions*, *Baudelaire* and *Saint-Genet*) are non-fiction, philosophical works. So although Barthes was far removed from the action of Nazi occupation and the subsequent liberation in France, he was, theoretically and intellectually, highly conversant with the debates and arguments that emerged in the war-weary but justice-hungry France of the immediate post-war period.

Barthes would remain friends with Fournié's wife, Jacqueline, for the rest of his life, and was by all accounts deeply affected by Fournié's death in 1968. In order to gauge the influence of Fournié's

Marxism on Barthes, one need only compare Barthes' writings immediately before meeting Fournié (mostly the pieces published in *Existences*), with those that immediately followed. Before August 1947 (the date of his first article on the 'degree zero' thesis in *Combat*), Barthes' writings, though perspicacious and sensitive in their ideas, were largely *belles-lettristes* – that is, concerned with literature and arts outside of social, political and ideological concerns. All this changed in the immediate post-war period, where a much more politicized self can be seen to emerge; from the article on the 'degree zero' thesis in 1947 onwards, Barthes' optic was quite clearly Marxist.[8]

It was then with some irony that Roland Barthes, the newly fashioned existentialist Marxist with Trotskyist leanings, who emerged in 1946, managed to find a post, thanks to his old school friend Philippe Rebeyrol, working as a librarian in the Institut français in newly Stalinist Romania. While waiting for the post to start in autumn 1947, Barthes signed up to write a thesis on Michelet with the Sorbonne professor René Pintard, but the project never came to academic fruition. More important for Barthes' career was the help his Trotskyist friend Fournié gave him by introducing him to Maurice Nadeau, also a former Trotskyist and now trying to forge a career as a journalist with the former Resistance newspaper founded by Albert Camus, *Combat*. A left-leaning but non-communist daily, *Combat* was the publication in which Camus first rejected Stalinism and in which Barthes wrote his first widely circulated article. This piece would, with five other pieces in *Combat* between 1947 and 1951, become the basis of his first book in 1953, *Writing Degree Zero*.[9]

Despite the interest raised by the first of these articles and by the one that followed in response to the voluminous correspondence the first had generated, Barthes was not able to convince Raymond Queneau, reader at Gallimard (and publisher of Camus and Sartre), to accept the book manuscript. In the end, it was thanks to Jean

Cayrol and Albert Béguin that Les Éditions du seuil – the left-leaning Catholic publisher that went on to support Barthes' books for the rest of his career – decided to include his essay in its Pierres vives series. The title of the series itself, which is written on the cover, is a quote from Montaigne: 'je ne bastis que pierres vives: ce sont hommes' (all I am building is living stones: they are men). One reason why Queneau may not have recommended Barthes' first book was that the 'degree zero' thesis performed, although only implicitly, a critique of Sartre's 'transparent' view of language. While in 1947 in *What is Literature?* Sartre maintained that literature could be politically committed irrespective of the language deployed, Barthes' thesis argued, against this, that literary form – the writer's attitude to his language – was indeed a crucial site of political commitment. It was a significant difference of approach to literary writing for Barthes, who was otherwise heavily influenced by Sartrian notions of intellectual commitment.

Barthes' mother accompanied Barthes to Romania in 1947, though his half-brother Michel did not. As part of the Université de Paris, the Institut français in Bucharest offered Barthes, once again, the chance to meet and work with a number of important academics and writers, such as Pierre Guiraud, a specialist in linguistics (and future tutor to Louis-Jean Calvet, Barthes' first biographer); Jean Sirinelli, the Hellenist; and Charles Singevin, a philosopher. He also took the opportunity to give lectures – on French *chanson* (Piaf, Montand and Trenet), and on Voltaire as someone born before the nineteenth century, the century of history.[10] Barthes' other duties included, once again, organizing the (well-stocked) library. Thus the sanatorium world, minus the fear of death, was reconstituted for him in Bucharest. But the relative calm and academic warmth there was contrasted with the unfolding events in Romania, which was slowly but surely becoming Stalinized into a one-party state, and which progressively became more anti-French as the Iron Curtain fell across Eastern Europe. The Institut français, much to Barthes' disappointment, was finally forced to close, and he was one of the last to leave as the library was packed up. In a final speech to the disappointed Romanians learning French there, Barthes played the music of Glück in order to illustrate his view that, despite (so-called) communism looking decidedly reactionary in its brutal ejection of French intellectuals from Romania as the Cold War set in, 'History could never deny its own march.'[11]

Barthes' overall positive experience of Bucharest was not, however, to be repeated when in 1949 he was next sent to Alexandria in Egypt. It was not that he failed to meet important people there – as a *lecteur* (reader) with Singevin, he worked with the newly qualified lecturer in the history of languages Algirdas Julien Greimas. Crucially, it was Greimas who initiated Barthes into the thought of Ferdinand de Saussure, and into semiology and structuralism more generally. Indeed, with Egyptian students on strike against King Farouk's corruption, Barthes, Greimas and Singevin had plenty of time for discussions. The growing importance of phenomenology was covered by Singevin's knowledge and interest in Husserl, by Barthes' reading of Sartre and by Greimas' appreciation of Maurice Merleau-Ponty. Greimas was fully conversant not only with Saussure, but with other 'early' structuralists, such as Roman Jakobson and Vigo Brøndal.

The main difference between Bucharest and Alexandria – or so it would seem – was the absence of his mother. While he was in Alexandria, she was looking after his eighteen-year-old half-brother Michel back in Paris, if only for the financial reasons that were entirely absent during Barthes' stay in Bucharest; namely, his mother needing to work in Paris to support Michel's studies for which Roland's salary in Egypt was not enough. It seems that Barthes would go on helping to support his half-brother financially for most of his life.[12] As we have noted, Marie Gil sees this preoccupation in the chosen title of his essay *S/Z*, and also in the essay's obsession with money: that giving Michel money was, in psychoanalytical terms, a confession of both Barthes' rejection of and an acceptance of the half-brother. Other family and personal issues began to mount for Barthes. According to Maurice Nadeau, Barthes' future was a cause for concern for his mother: Barthes was so close to her, so fragile, so different from his half-brother, at a time when homosexuality in France had to be hidden.[13] Though Egypt was less stimulating intellectually and socially than Romania, it would seem Barthes' homosexuality was more open in Egypt.

Barthes maintained links with *Combat*, writing a report from Karnak on the debates raging between Egyptologists in the late 1940s, which he also gave as a lecture in Paris when he returned in June 1950.[14] During the period of 1948–50, he also wrote a second series of articles on the 'degree zero' thesis, which *Combat* published in 1950 and 1951. None of this was enough to make up for his interrupted academic career, however, and once again, it was Rebeyrol who helped him to obtain a post, this time at the cultural relations department of the French Foreign Affairs Ministry in Paris. Between 1950 and 1953, while working in the Foreign Affairs Ministry office, Barthes was trying to establish a career and had little time for his own work. Thanks to Greimas, Barthes was invited by Georges Matoré in 1951 to work on Georges Gougenheim's essential French vocabulary project, but he failed to complete it. (In the end, the list of 2,000 essential French words was published, without Barthes' input, by Didier in 1958.) This turned out to be just one of a number of 'false starts' in Barthes' career during the 1950s. He toyed with the idea of a book on France for Hachette, and also hesitated before finally declining *lecteur* posts in both Cambridge and Bologna. As Barthes began to be noticed in this early 1950s period, he made one more decision: to leave the Foreign Affairs Ministry and to try to get a research post in the burgeoning area of social sciences. Greimas obliged again, helping Barthes this time to become a trainee in lexicology at the Centre national de la recherche scientifique (cnrs), working with

Charles Bruneau. In 1952 he was awarded a grant by the CNRS for a thesis on socio-linguistics and lexicology, considering the vocabulary of political and social economics in France between 1825 and 1835. However, Barthes' commitment to his 'degree zero' essay and to his work on Michelet prevented him from making enough progress for his CNRS grant to be renewed in 1953.

In spite of these 'false starts', articles by Barthes began to appear in this period. Book reviews for *Combat* were published in 1951, as well as a lengthy piece on Michelet's historiography in *Esprit*, the Catholic journal whose political activities were very much left-wing existentialist, and with which, temporarily, Barthes was happy to be involved. It was at *Esprit* that Barthes met Jean Cayrol, a Bordeaux poet before the war who, after returning from the Mauthausen concentration camp, was now trying to rebuild his life by specifically rejecting poetry and instead exploring the post-war novel and its experiments. It is easy to underestimate Cayrol's importance in the French post-war literary scene. However, in the 1950s and '60s, he was the key player behind the launch of the radical 1960s journal *Tel Quel*, having 'found' and encouraged Philippe Sollers (among others) in the mid-1950s and organized the writing project *Écrire*. Barthes' impressive study of Cayrol's novels appeared in *Esprit* in 1952, and Barthes worked closely with the concentration-camp survivor on a number of projects.[15] The importance of writing in the camps was in its collective act, in the secrecy of the camp latrines, in a bizarre, even macabre foretaste of the writing *atelier* (workshop), which, though resembling the 'Oxford of the Alps' sanatorium for Barthes, was a stark and cruel reminder of literature at 'the midnight of the century'. Following Cayrol's experiences in the concentration camps, the deepest hole that humanity had fallen into, Barthes could begin to consider writing as a (deeply) social act; this encouraged Barthes to read Cayrol's post-war novels as the beginning of a new sociality for humanity, a new station, post-Auschwitz.

One other key development in the world of publishing and intellectual journalism in the early 1950s for Barthes was the demise of *Combat* and the invitation from Maurice Nadeau to join the newly launched weekly *Observateur*. Nadeau asked Barthes to contribute to a survey of 'left-wing literature', which allowed Barthes to befriend the ex-Communist Party member and writer of a history of death Edgar Morin.[16] However, this was but a stepping stone for Nadeau, who, with Maurice Saillet, later created a new left-wing monthly journal, *Les Lettres nouvelles*. It was in the pages of this monthly journal, between 1954 and 1956, that Barthes began his study of myth and the ideological distortions operated by the mass culture developing in 1950s France.

In line with Gide's fascination with natural science and with Michelet's writings on nature, Barthes' writings during the period 1947–52 referred regularly to a much-debated animal, the duck-billed platypus. This most biologically curious of animals wandered into essays and book reviews by Barthes in *Combat*, acting as an example of the scandalously unclassifiable, of a creature that had defied natural scientists' attempts at classification for centuries.[17] This interest in singularity – with the exceptional, with that which breaks (or at least shows the limits to) classification – may seem at odds with the social dimension of Barthes' writing and theory. But the platypus perfectly illustrated the point, which would be borne out throughout Barthes' career, that to posit a structure (a classification, a definition, a position) was equally to posit its undermining, its oscillating opposite, its ruin.

Throughout his career, Barthes had sought to paint social phenomena – including the self, himself – in their (tightly held) structures, only to then, like Houdini, collapse the opposing elements that made up the structures. In the same way, the platypus had defied those scientists, from Linnaeus in the eighteenth century onwards, who could not handle its mammalian but oviparous body. Indeed, borrowing Vigo Brøndal's notion of a 'third term' (marked, unmarked and then the neutral), Barthes deployed the 'degree zero' thesis as a (utopian) way of breaking, or going beyond, the binary. It is for this reason that Marie Gil uses the psychoanalytically inspired figure of the 'hole' into which Barthes was placed (or indeed, into which he placed himself). Though this is a deeply and impressively 'parametric' approach (placing Barthes' psychic disposition and drives in dialogue with his own theoretical and writerly enterprise of establishing and then breaking structures), Gil's approach runs the risk of a tight circularity that reduces all Barthesian theory to the person Barthes. Both of Barthes' first two books, *Writing Degree Zero* and *Michelet*, seemed, in some way, to contradict this individualist, self-preoccupied image.

The 'degree zero' thesis, as set out in articles between 1947 and 1951 and in the final book version published in 1953 as *Writing Degree Zero*, underlined the social nature of literary language, albeit alienated into a literary 'institution' as a guarantee of its literariness. Though not highlighted by critics, the 'degree zero' thesis explicitly regretted the manner in which the bourgeoisie's control of French language, since the mid-seventeenth century, had excluded the *homme populaire*, the ordinary French person, from discourse. This concern with 'ordinary' people was repeated in Barthes' appreciation of Michelet's history writing.

If Barthes' fascination with Michelet was beholden to the way in which the Romantic historian had been able to articulate his own bodily experiences through his history writing, this was but a part of the social way in which Michelet had approached his subject: the people, specifically the French, were to be embodied in national(ist) history writing. Michelet claimed that his (magisterial) nineteen-volume history of France was 'himself' reflected; it was not an arrogant, conceited or self-preoccupied promotion of himself, but a selfless offering of his writing person to 'resurrect', to provide a voice for, the 'masses' – the overwhelming majority of the world's population who have walked the planet but have been excluded from 'official' history. All of Michelet's writing – even the frank and graphic diaries of his marital difficulties – could be seen as a way of inscribing the silent minions of history into social discourse: no event, no person, no phenomenon failed to be indicative of those nameless (often faceless) monads that 'people' history and mean that the historian is 'dissolved' into them. Indeed, Barthes quoted Michelet, in his early piece on the *Journal* of André Gide in *Existences* in 1942, likening Gide's diary writing to Michelet's view of his history writing in his 1869 preface to his *History of France*: 'History . . . makes the historian much more than it is made by him. My book has created me. I am its work.'[18]

As well as keenly and accurately identifying Michelet's obsessions as the organizing principles in his history and natural science writing, Barthes also showed that Michelet was a visual as well as visionary writer. Michelet was one of the first modern historians to see and deeply regret what the working-class historian E. P. Thompson would call, a century later, the 'enormous condescension of posterity'. At the same time, Michelet was fascinated by one area that seemed to allude to this 'populocentric' picture: the natural world, especially the Insect, but also the Sea, the Bird and even (rather controversially for today's gender politics) the Woman. Nevertheless, Barthes suggested that Michelet's attitude towards the binary of gender was ahead of his time, as Michelet was shown by Barthes to have 'both sexes of the mind' (used as the epigraph in Barthes' *Michelet*). Michelet was attuned to both genders' experiences, collapsing and overcoming divisions, and questioning the marking of structured identity and social function in gender well before Edward Carpenter. This would be a key element in Barthes' reading of Balzac's story 'Sarrasine' in *s/z* in the late 1960s; indeed, Michelet's belief in his ability to be (attuned to) both man and woman was a *social* attempt at human unity.

Barthes' book *Michelet* was published in 1954 by Seuil in the Par lui-même series, which, as well as allowing each writer to be quoted at length alongside biographical commentaries, was amply illustrated in each of its many volumes. Indeed, Éditions du seuil's Par lui-même series is very similar to the Critical Lives series in which Reaktion Books has published this present book. Barthes was fascinated by the way in which (painted) portraits suggested a 'character' of the painted subject to Michelet. One might say this was a deeply 'individualist' approach (in both senses – individual to the subject in the portrait, and individualist in the subjective attribution given by any one viewer), but this would be to miss the role of 'Image' in modern society. Importantly, Barthes was suggesting – in other essays on Michelet at the time – that, as much as one may act in history, this was no guarantee of how this action would then be interpreted across history, and even that the historical 'meaning' of a human actant, or actants, was relative: it can change with new interpretations brought about by a new vantage point in the future, and is, of course, therefore infinite. (Joan of Arc would be a good example of such a deeply polyvalent historical character.)[19] This mobility of image was to become a key element in Barthes' later work. Much of Barthes' sociological writing in the mid-1950s – on children in advertising, on the human face in a cinema-star-saturated world, on clothing at work and then in fashion – was an interrogation of how we react (usually, passively) to image-construction.[20] We will return to Barthes' sociological approach to image in *Mythologies* and to ideology in general in the next chapter. It is important now to suggest how Barthes' very first book, *Writing Degree Zero*, fitted into this sociological framework.

The opening words of *Writing Degree Zero*, in the introduction, have often been misunderstood as Barthes flagrantly contradicting the very thesis of the book.[21] To say that the French Revolution was such a big upheaval that it can be seen even in the bawdy and crude language that revolutionary newspapers suddenly felt free to use was one thing; and yet the rest of *Writing Degree Zero* tried to show how writers – especially those in the modern period, since Flaubert in the 1850s onwards – had tried to deploy their own language that could (or could seem to) deftly escape determination by history. Thus the examples of bad language in Hébert's revolutionary newspaper in Barthes' preface seemed to flatly contradict this as sharp examples of how exactly 'history' inflects language choice. We saw above how Barthes' presentation of Michelet underscored the dialectical – that is, oscillatory rather than contradictory – nature of 'meaning' in and across history. Simply put, the swear word appearing in revolutionary newspapers in 1790s France can be understood, following Barthes' analysis, in two generic ways: first, it can be seen as galvanizing the Revolution *at the time*, pushing it forward even in the language used during it; secondly, *across history*, swearing 'signals' the Revolution to us from afar. Language thus 'acts', Barthes was implying, because it shakes up the accepted norms of late eighteenth-century society. But this language also tells us that it *has* acted – our 'enormous condescension of posterity' allows us to see, from our vantage point, that language has had a historical (and not just revolutionary-communicative) function. We are talking here then about the historical and sociological contest *within* language; in the swear words example of the 'degree zero' thesis, the contest seems to be resolved. But when it comes to clothing forms across history (the new research project that Barthes developed across the 1950s following *Michelet* and *Writing Degree Zero*), clothing seemed to escape this dialectic of acting and then meaning. It was an important philosophical lesson then that Barthes felt unable to 'read' social upheaval in changes of clothing and fashion, prefer-ring to see changes in human apparel as part of 'slow' sociological developments (involving social class, mass media and ideological function), rather than as the effect of a stark historical event. This is not to say that Barthes ignored this question in his first book. Indeed, the schema in *Writing Degree Zero*'s history of writing and literary language saw a similar phenomenon in the French language.

One of the key points was Barthes' emphasis – despite his swear words example in the introduction – that the French Revolution, contrary to popular belief, actually changed precious little in French literary language, in how a writer selected words and put them together; instead, it was the 1848 revolution, fifty years later, Barthes argued, that had cracked open the writers' unproblematic use of language as a 'medium', thus leading to the modern (utopian) search for a 'degree zero' of language that precisely could *not* be seen differently depending on whether one was reading Camus in 1942 or in 2015. In other words, the rest of the 'degree zero' thesis was a rejection of the swear words phenomenon of 1790s France in the new post-1848 world of 'modern writing'; whereas the former could be both a historical act at the time (swearing in revolutionary France acted upon history) *and* a signal to us across time of this transgression, the French language, following the events of 1848, by contrast, could no longer sustain this dual function (or if it did, the two were not working harmoniously in the way Barthes suggested they had been up until 1848). Barthes used the *longue durée* (long duration) approach to explain the hegemony of bourgeois thought since the seventeenth century's standardization of 'French', even suggesting that France was 'internally colonized' by this upper-class, 'bourgeois' language developed around Paris in Port Royal grammars and 'imposed' between 1650 and 1850 in a long-term bid to form the bourgeois French nation-state. But crucially, this language had become problematic, socially fissured, not when newspapers used swear words during the French Revolution, but when writers realized, fifty years later, that bourgeois thought was anything but 'universalist'. Despite its universalist pretensions in and through language (the French Revolution having finally brought to political power the bourgeoisie, who had already built up ideological and economic power, partly thanks to the unification of France via its standardized language), the French language, following the events of 1848, was shown to be thoroughly bourgeois and partisan to this now-dominant social class; in short, the 'red days' of the 1848 uprising in France, when the red flag was first raised, proved that bourgeois rule was a class rule, that language was class-biased towards the ruling class. Swearing after 1848 could no longer have the effect at the time that it had done in 1790s France – such was the 'recuperation' of language as modernity took hold in the 1850s, especially in literature, where it could be 'contained' as part of Literature, as part of the bourgeois literary 'institution'. (Just look at how, for example, James Joyce's debauched language is accommodated today.)

Two conclusions can be drawn from our 'social' discussion of the 'degree zero' thesis. First, literature – all writing, all speech acts and especially all literature because it claims the greatest freedom of all language acts – is part of an 'institution'. Here is one half of the swear words dialectic: for language to be 'literary', it has to signal itself as such (there are numerous ways of doing this, of course). However, the other half of the swear word dialectic no longer seemed to pertain: if literary language is necessarily 'recuperated' (accommodated, nullified) by dint of its signalling its place in the 'literary institution', can one's use of language (as Hébert had shown) change anything? Not only was this a challenge to Sartre's view that *littérature engagée* (politically committed literature) could only come through a transparent use of language (and ignoring the ideological functions of its many forms), it suggested that Barthes was working against simplistic resolutions of conflicting ideas. Here we see the start of Barthes' open-ended dialectic: contradictory phenomena could exist alongside each other without the need to resolve dialectically into something new. Such a questioning of Hegel's rigorous three-part dialectic, in which the clash of thesis and antithesis leads to a newness that emerges from and in their antagonistic synthesis (Hébert's swear words both act at the time *and* signal across history to produce a synthetic – even unified – view of language during and since the French Revolution, a unity that suits the bourgeoisie's claims to a 'universalist' language when it patently is not), was to become a trademark approach for the oscillating Barthes: never synthesizing, but always in motion, shuttling back and forth, as if, in Gil's psychoanalytical schema, falling into and then constantly climbing out of a hole between structure and its undoing, its over-coming. In this sense then, Barthes' first two books were deeply social: they examined history writing and literary writing in their fundamentally wide-ranging sociological and historical functions in and across society and societies.

The year 1953 was an important year for Barthes and his family. Not only did 1953 see Barthes publish his first book, it was the year his family's fortunes changed radically. Following the death of Noémi Révelin, her considerable estate was split between Henriette and Henriette's brother Philippe, now living in Canada (Étienne having died in 1945). Not only did Barthes benefit from an inheritance thanks to the sale of the family foundry in eastern France, but he received a rather elegant, if old-fashioned, Panhard car and the holiday house in Hendaye. Suddenly, the family that had struggled to make ends meet at the end of every month was able to experience luxury or, at least, financial ease.[22] Barthes even lived with his mother for a short time in Noémi's prestigious flat in the Place du Panthéon in central Paris. Noémi had already proved a very useful connection in the 1930s, as we saw with Paul Valéry and his support of the student Barthes in the 1930s. Her importance now was that she had removed a key source of social alienation – the embarrassment of impecuniousness – and had allowed the forty-year-old Barthes to stop panicking about a singular lack of career. However, if the experience of socio-economic alienation had been largely removed by 1954, the other main pressure on Barthes' life – his sexuality and sexual identity – could not be expressed openly, especially in this 1950s period of orthodox gender relations and the restoration of male/female distinctions following the blurring of genders during the Second World War. (Indeed, *Mythologies* contains a number of fascinating critiques of gender politics in France in the 1950s, from children's toys to women's magazines and female novelists). It was not then a coincidence that Barthes should in this period attempt to go into psychoanalytical treatment, approaching, but being rejected by, Jacques Lacan in 1954. His meeting that year and deep friendship with Bernard Dort, with whom he shared a passion for theatre, was a temporary solution to his personal difficulties. Dort would also introduce Barthes to the work of some pioneering artists: first Alain Robbe-Grillet and then Bertolt Brecht. This was to become a rather strange combination of two very different writers to enthuse over – one deeply suspicious of the novel's claim to have political efficacy, the other deeply committed to a radical aesthetics in the theatre. Yet both were maverick and original enough to warrant Barthes' attention and, ultimately, his critical support.

3

Marxism, Popular Theatre and the New Novel

Initiation into Marxist theory, combined with a highly charged radical moment in France between 1944 and 1948 and illustrated by the rise of Sartre's philosophy of existentialism and intellectual 'responsibility', in turn gave rise, as we have seen, to Barthes' first major series of theoretical essays, the 'degree zero' theory of literature (1947–53). These years were to be crucial in founding Barthes' own writerly, intellectual commitment to social justice, heavily influenced by Sartre's situated 'ethos'; and though Barthes differed sharply from Sartre over his attitude to language, the overall Sartrian idea of the writer as activist became the guiding light for the rest of Barthes' career.

The years 1953 and 1954 were a turning point in Barthes' early career. Not only did his financial situation start to look up with the death of his wealthy maternal grandmother, Noémi, but *Writing Degree Zero* was very well received. *Michelet* too was given good press, especially by the eminent historian Lucien Febvre, who could see that Barthes had spotted Michelet's obsessions from his published writings and that Barthes' intuitive reading was to be corroborated in Michelet's diaries, which Febvre was editing in 1954.

In 1954, thanks to the inheritance from Noémi, Barthes, his mother and his half-brother moved into a modest but well-located flat in the rue Servandoni at the edge of the Latin Quarter in Paris, where Barthes was able to have his own room and office upstairs through a trapdoor. Located on a side street off Saint-Sulpice, in the sixth arrondissement of Paris, Barthes' flat was but two steps away from the Café de Flore, from Saint-Germain-des-Prés and from the Left Bank intellectual culture associated with Sartre, Simone de Beauvoir and others. However, if the family finances were suddenly and incontrovertibly stable, Barthes' career was not at all. In 1954 he had two respected books under his belt but no actual career. Attempts at launching a researcher's trajectory were all met with closed doors because Barthes did not have a PhD. In 1955, as we have seen, his CNRS grant was not renewed, despite a letter of support from the philosopher Gaston Bachelard. Fortunately Georges Friedmann, supported by Febvre and Braudel, managed to obtain a post in sociology for him, for a project on *les signes et les symboles sociaux dans les relations humaines* (signs and social symbols in human relations) at the newly created Centre d'études sociologiques (CES), as part of the larger programme on the history of clothing and vestimentary mythology led by Friedmann.

Barthes' knowledge of sociology was patchy, but this was hardly surprising given the burgeoning nature of the subject in this post-war period: Werner Sombart, Gilberto Freyre, Bernard Groethuysen, Émile Durkheim, Marcel Mauss and Georges Gurvitch – not to mention Claude Lévi-Strauss's structural anthropology – were minor but significant sociological influences on Barthes' early career. He was also an avid reader of the *Annales*, the journal of the history grouping of the same name, which was one of the first in modern academia to mix history with sociology. Furthermore, through Lucien Febvre's stewardship, there was a direct link between the *Annales* and Jules Michelet's writings – in 1954 not only was Febvre working on Michelet's diaries and correspondence, but Michelet's susceptibility to notions of social totality, to physical and material experiences and to the experience of the masses were key influences on the *Annales* historians. In addition Barthes had unwittingly assimilated the great nineteenth-century historian's voluminous writings into his intellectual, rhetorical and writerly outlook, even to the point that Michelet's (progressive) populism – his most famous essay was that on *Le Peuple* (The People) in 1845 – undeniably played a role in Barthes' work on popular culture in the 1950s.

There was during this uncertain but formative period of Barthes' life in the mid-1950s one other highly formative experience, extensive as much as it is profound for Barthes: his activism. Between 1953 and 1959, he took part in the burgeoning popular theatre movement, which, since the liberation of France and especially the Avignon Festival's launch in 1947, had been working across France to bring more than the 'usual' 2 per cent of the population to the theatre. Not only did Barthes work tirelessly with the Théâtre national populaire (TNP) and its national members' organization the Amis du théâtre populaire (ATP) – drumming up support for sophisticated, well-chosen and intelligently designed productions that were financially and geographically accessible to the 'masses' – Barthes was invited in 1954 onto the editorial board of what was to become one of the most influential theatre journals of the twentieth century, appropriately (if confusingly) also called *Théâtre populaire*, which was entirely independent of the TNP. Launched by André Voisin, a Germanist fellow traveller of the French Communist Party, *Théâtre populaire* was produced by the left-wing publisher L'Arche, which was busy translating German drama into French (especially the radical theatre of Bertolt Brecht), but also crucially – at least in the early stages – supporting the aims and policies of mass theatre culture in France led by the TNP and its actor-director Jean Vilar.

A regular visitor to the wrestling bouts at the Elysée Montmartre theatre in northern Paris, Barthes had written a piece in *Esprit* in 1952 on this most popular and working-class of spectacles (which became the first essay, 'The World of Wrestling', in *Mythologies* in 1957), in which wrestling's sport status was replaced by its theatrical and popular dimensions. More akin to ancient Greek

Cover of the issue of *Théâtre populaire* featuring Barthes' article on avant-garde theatre.

theatre, wrestling in 1950s France, argued Barthes, was not about physical feats of power and skill, but about the signs of justice and audience participation in the construction of the image of justice. One must contrast his enthusiasm for wrestling with his article the following year, also in *Esprit*, on the Folies Bergère club in Paris; in it, he vehemently criticized the music hall's sickly, petit bourgeois and passive-making effect on the audience, in contrast to wrestling's demand for audience participation, for grander notions of justice and for a clarity in the artifice being employed.[1]

As well as being impressed by this piece on wrestling, Voisin appreciated Barthes' review of the TNP's production of Heinrich von

Kleist's tender tragedy *Le Prince de Hombourg*, which was published in Nadeau's new monthly journal *Les Lettres nouvelles*.[2] Thus Barthes was invited to become, for a short period, a 'literary advisor' at L'Arche publishing house (handily located on Place Saint-Sulpice near his house) while co-editing – and, at some stages in 1954 and 1955, editing alone – the in-house journal *Théâtre populaire*.[3] Championing first the directing and acting style adopted by the TNP's eminent leader Jean Vilar and recommended for the rest of the popular theatre movement in France, Barthes – soon to be accompanied by Bernard Dort – was subsequently 'blown away' by the arrival in Paris of the Berliner Ensemble and their performance of Brecht's anti-war play *Mother Courage*. At a time when France had been brutally defeated in its first post-war war of decolonization in Indochina (in what we might call the 'first' Vietnam War of 1945 to 1954) and was about to sink into the even bloodier conflict against the anti-colonial uprising that began in Algeria in November 1954, Barthes and Dort were swiftly converted to Brecht's epic theatre as an aesthetic for the masses that encouraged them, according to *Théâtre populaire* in 1954 and 1955, to take history into their own hands. In a series of (unsigned) editorials in the journal, Barthes swiftly rejected Aristotelian theatre – tragedy, for the most part – as an inappropriate theatre aesthetic for the modern world. He contrasted Brecht's austere but politically charged attempts to inspire in the audience a critical distance between themselves and the action on the stage with the bourgeois theatre of the *boulevard* in Paris and its complacent and patronizing relation with the audience.[4]

Both Barthes and Dort were pilloried for their communist-leaning preference for Brechtian theatre, in the midst of the Cold War, and were made the object of theatrical satire in Eugène Ionesco's rather dire one-act play of 1956, *L'Impromptu de l'Alma* (Improvisation at Alma), in which the characters – all called Bartholoméus, in a direct reference to Barthes, and numbered

I to III – parodied Brecht's injunctions to his actors to 'distance' themselves from the part they were playing. Though Barthes and Dort were both principled and brave in their staunch defence and promotion of Brecht's theatre, it would not be unfair to say that Brecht's theatre arrived in France at a time when the popular theatre movement was slowly beginning to lose steam (and funding), being unable to sustain a true people's theatre.

It is clear that this experience presented a steep learning curve for Barthes, not just in how to run (that is, to edit and put together) a journal, but in answering the question of whether such popular theatre was possible under capitalist social and ideological relations. Though the experience was overall a hugely positive one – not least because Brecht became a major theoretical influence on him – Barthes had left popular theatre by the end of the 1950s with the distinct impression that alienated cultural reality necessarily precluded a truly mass, popular theatre: either the choice of play risked trivializing the grandeur of theatre (Barthes was acutely aware of this as a scholar of ancient Greek culture and founder of the Sorbonne student theatre group in the 1930s), or the day-to-day drudgery of work for the vast majority of the population discouraged sustained communion with the 'high' culture of theatre. Alternatively, perhaps the production style – syrupy and simplistic – merely patronized the audience and played to the lowest common denominator of critical involvement.

Crucially for Barthes, having set out the recipe for successful popular theatre in various articles and speeches around France in 1954, it was clear by 1958 that the three vital elements in this recipe – a sophisticated repertoire of plays, an audience of 'ordinary' people and an innovative approach to production styles – were a tall order for a nationalized theatre movement.[5] The election (and return) of General Charles de Gaulle in 1958, and the subsequent appointment of novelist André Malraux to the head of the Ministry of Culture, sounded the death knell for the potential of popular theatre in France.

Indeed, one of Malraux's first initiatives was to 'decentralize' theatre by creating a network of *maisons de la culture* in the major towns and cities across France; this was seen by Barthes as a form of state control, recuperating and harnessing the energy of popular theatre into the technocratic modernization of France. It is no coincidence then that Barthes attended the demonstrations ten years later, in early 1968, against Malraux's heavy-handed sacking of the anti-establishment leader of the Cinemathèque in Paris, Henri Langlois. These demonstrations were part of a militant movement that is widely seen as a catalyst to the May '68 uprising against Gaullism.

Barthes had made many new friends and acquaintances in the popular theatre movement, the most important being Bernard Dort, with whom he shared not just a passion for theatre, but a love of cooking and cigars. Barthes' trademark cigar was the Punch Culbras (beloved of Brecht and Lacan), and following his inheritance in 1954, he could afford to become a bit indulgent. Dort, too, was gay, at a time when homosexuality was tolerated but illegal in France. Dort and Barthes also shared an interest in the novel, specifically in the *nouveau roman*, as it was quickly dubbed, exemplified by Alain Robbe-Grillet, and for which Cayrol was a precursor. For Barthes, as the theorist of the (utopian) degree zero of writing, the *nouveau roman* did not solve the conundrum of blank writing's signifying 'literary' in a literature institution that was beholden to a society in which bourgeois-dominated language seemed all-pervasive. But the critique of plot, of character and of romantic notions of nature seemingly operated by the *nouveau roman* was, for Barthes, a step in the right direction, towards what he called a 'cleansing' of all that was compromised and reactionary in the 1950s novel.[6] Interestingly, Barthes defended the *nouveau roman* against its (numerous) detractors by emphasizing the 'literalness' typical of its style, and rejecting the metaphorical readings that were heaped on Robbe-Grillet's novels. Yet a decade later in 1965, when Barthes defended 'new criticism' against the traditionalist Sorbonne professor Raymond Picard, he would criticize Picard and others precisely for their literalism – another example of Barthes occupying a position later in his career that he had roundly rejected and criticized at another, earlier stage.

If the *nouveau roman* represented for Barthes a 'cleansing' of (though, importantly, not an alternative to) bourgeois literary aesthetics, then it was Brecht's epic theatre that offered this solution. Barthes had, as we saw, begun his career in the popular theatre movement extolling the virtues of tragedy; following his reading of Nietzsche during the war, he had appreciated tragedy as a crucial element for a theatre that could speak to the people in difficult times (and post-war France had plenty of reason for 'tragedy', be it the fallout from the civil war that ended the Nazi occupation, or the brutal and cruel wars of decolonization that stretched and divided France and its empire from 1945 to 1962). However, Barthes then discovered, as if in a religious conversion, the epic theatre promoted by Brecht. The excitement that Brechtian theatre brought to dramaturgy (in Britain too) eclipsed the enthusiasm for Samuel Beckett's *Waiting for Godot* (first performed in Paris in 1953), and Brechtian theatre was rapidly advocated as the solution to the travails of the TNP, which, by 1955, was beginning to falter in its mission to bring a high-culture repertoire of plays performed with an avant-garde production style to the masses. Barthes' (unsigned) editorials in *Théâtre populaire* during 1954 and 1955 were consequently the most militant of his career, indicative of his (and Dort's) enthusiasm for the distancing effect of Brecht's plays on the audience and the subsequent 'critical' position that the spectators were encouraged to develop. However, the vituperative editorials also betrayed a creeping desperation and dissatisfaction with the overall direction of the popular theatre movement, as the TNP movement's leader Jean Vilar was criticized as both actor and director for pandering to bourgeois theatre's values and ideologies.[7] Inevitably, this led to a number of squabbles over Brechtian theatre, in which Dort and Barthes were the stalwart defenders of the German playwright. Soon Barthes and Dort were casting around the French popular-theatre movement to find the French Brecht. The director Roger Planchon, whose theatre in the suburbs of Lyon was attracting working-class audiences, was one inspiring example, and the young playwright Michel Vinaver was, for a time, influenced by Brechtian categories in his early dramas, such as *Aujourd'hui*.[8]

It is near-impossible to overestimate both the significance of the general experience of the popular theatre experience for Barthes (running a journal and being an activist) and the discovery of Brechtian theory in particular. These further inspired Barthes' early interest in photography – he wrote a fascinating commentary in 1958 on the photographic record of the Berliner Ensemble's visit and production in Paris in 1954 made by the radical photographer Roger Pic.[9] More widely, Barthes appreciated Brecht for being a rare artist: a Marxist who reflected on the effects of the sign.[10] At exactly the same time that he was promoting Brecht as the cure for the ills of the popular theatre movement, Barthes was defending and extolling the virtues of the *nouveau roman*, using his skills in essayism and literary criticism. One further dimension needs to be added to this essay writing, literary criticism and theatre activism: his regular monthly column between 1954 and 1956 in Nadeau's journal *Les Lettres nouvelles*, called 'La Petite mythologie du mois' (Small Mythologies of the Month), written in a series of short essays (usually between one and five pieces per month, depending on length). When collected, these were to become the backbone of his broadside from 1957 against bourgeois ideological persuasion, *Mythologies*. Typical of Barthes' writing career, this book was made up of pieces that had mostly been published elsewhere – mainly in *Les Lettres nouvelles*, but also in *Esprit*.

We have not, so far, underlined the deeply social nature of his experiences and the theories that he developed during his extended activism in the popular theatre movement. Theatre being a collective experience par excellence, Barthes' social investment in it was augmented by the editorial collective that he organized for the *Théâtre populaire* journal and by the ATP meetings and functions in which he was active between 1954 and 1956. This social experience left a deep impression on *Mythologies*, and not just in the pieces on theatre in the collection – those that look at drama by Arthur Adamov, at the theatre of Jean Racine, at Marxist critic Henri Lefebvre's theatre criticism, at new and young theatre, and at the music hall – but in the political implications and conclusions of the final essay, to which we will come in a moment. Above all, Barthes' main optic in *Mythologies* was a deeply social, sociological one. Indeed (and this should be no surprise given our discussion in Chapter Two of the 'internal colonization' that the 'degree zero' thesis saw bourgeois language foisting on the French masses), it was an attempt to get inside the acts of *self*-persuasion that the French mind – as a collective, social entity – was constantly operating in the new era of mass media and communication that characterized the 1950s. I italicize the 'self' in 'self-persuasion' because there is a certain amount of confusion or conflation in accounts of Barthes' *Mythologies*.

In *Mythologies* Barthes used, for the first time, his growing interest in semiology – the science of communication – although this was not to show that reality was twisted and distorted, full of myths subliminally encouraging us to purchase (as the American theorist of advertising Vance Packard does in *The Hidden Persuaders*, also published in 1957), nor even to show (as Richard Hoggart does in *Uses of Literacy*, also from 1957) that popular culture, mass culture, was becoming devalued by a cheap (often American-based) shallow culture. Rather, Barthes' *Mythologies* was a form of social psychoanalysis that looked at the way in which our minds – in a bid to give ourselves some kind of meaning, purpose and even disalienation – actively participated in self-delusions. Barthes made no attempt to deny that he was as caught up in this process of self-delusion as anyone else. Indeed, Dort apparently encouraged him to write (in the summer of 1956, while holidaying together in south-western France) the final, summative essay of *Mythologies*, 'Myth Today', as an *auto-mythologie* of himself. This was not the first time Barthes had ironized his own intellectual position – in 1955 he had accused Camus' allegory *La Peste* of having ignored real experiences. (Brechtian theatre was clearly being imported into his novel criticism here.)[11] Then, following his public argument with Camus over literalism and allegory in the novel, Barthes was in turn accused by the Gallimard mover and shaker Jean Paulhan (under the pseudonym Jean Guérin), as editor of a rival journal to *Les Lettres nouvelles*, of being a 'Marxist'. Having defended Sartre's play *Nekrassov* (1955) – a critique of Western journalists in the Cold War – against the baying theatre press who wanted Sartre's scalp, Barthes 'replied' to Guérin's (or Paulhan's) attribution of political beliefs in another *mythologie* in *Les Lettres nouvelles*, which was provocatively called 'Suis-je marxiste?' (Am I a Marxist?) but was, unfortunately, not included in the book.[12]

Following the 51 studies in *Mythologies*, it was, however, 'Myth Today' that was the most instrumental in moving Barthes' self-analysis onto a new terrain. Could Barthes the mythologist enjoy wine – be 'inside' it – while, at the same time, stepping 'outside' of wine and criticizing its deeply distorting ideological and mythical effects? And just to prove that he was as implicated in self-delusion as anyone else, he asked whether there was a myth of the mythologist. The social and political dead end that *Mythologies* described – whereby myth was all powerful in its ability to latch onto any phenomenon, including the mythologist – left open one possibility for action: writing. As a penetrating critique of Western mass culture in which self-delusion was the key component,

Mythologies seemed to suggest that writing alone could break the domination of our minds by mystification; this writing implied an affinity – not a distaste – with the very objects that seemed to encourage self-delusion. Therefore it is egregious in the extreme to suggest that Barthes did not 'like' any of the objects upon which he brought his Marxian-Brechtian analysis to bear in *Mythologies*. With the possible exception of the classical theatre of Jean Racine (France's equivalent to Shakespeare, if only in his standing, to whom we will return in Chapter Four), who is critiqued in *Mythologies* no doubt as a vestige of Barthes' passionate search for an appropriate popular theatre dramatist in French who could be the next Brecht, all the other objects that Barthes analysed in *Mythologies* held an ambivalent (ambiguous) attraction to him. In other words, Barthes (and the mythologist in general) was as implicated in (French) culture as anyone else, and the conclusion of *Mythologies* was keen to underline it. This, as Barthes saw it, was part of the problem. Short of living the life of a monk or nun, of excluding oneself, hermit-like, from the day-to-day operations of ideological and social alienation, everyone had to live – and 'consume' – in a world of Omo, Unilever, *Elle* and Minou Drouet.

Nevertheless, *Mythologies* did point to places of exit, even utopian insulation, from myth. Whether in wrestling, music-hall acrobatics or natural disasters such as floods in Paris, Barthes could glimpse moments in which the social order, on which myth was predicated, was undermined, temporarily broken down or suspended, in what we might call examples of 'happy' myths. The key point for Barthes was a Brechtian one, made clear in the opening essay on wrestling – that a healthy sign, of which there did not seem to be many in 1950s France, was an open, self-aware and ostentatious one. The wrestlers might not really hurt each other, but the audience wanted all the signs of justice, just desserts and fairness (the hero beating the villain, usually) to be clearly signified in a clarity that dominated the whole performance (including personalities, clothing and actions). But what did it mean to apply these Brechtian categories – designed, after all, for theatrical purposes – to real-life situations and social phenomena? Brecht, as a playwright and theatre director, was fully aware that as soon as his audience, critically positioned by the distancing effect of his epic theatre, left the theatre for the bright lights of the real world outside, their critical distance seeped away almost instantaneously before the realities of social life and its self-deluding alienation. Barthes' equivalent then would be writing: could he write in such a way that the reader – like Brecht's audience – could achieve a 'critical distance'? What would this mean when his readership – again, like Brecht's audience – left the 'theatre' of his essay writing for the bright lights of reality outside? Barthes' answer to this was to emerge across the 1960s: the reader (must?) become a writer himself, and all (of his) writing should foster more writing. This was precisely the lesson that Barthes had learned (if we remember from Chapter Two) in his reading of Gide: it made him want to write.

Mythologies proved a huge success, overall, for Barthes. It is true that it was beaten in 1958 for the Prix Sainte-Beuve by Emil Cioran's Nietzschean aphorisms *La Tentation d'exister* (The Temptation to Exist), but only by nine votes to seven. Furthermore, the wide press coverage – favourable on the Left, highly unfavourable on the Right – was enough to make Barthes into an intellectual of important standing in France in the late 1950s, evidenced by the fact that *Mythologies* was read widely over the next ten years, right up to the events of May 1968. One of the reasons for this success was that Barthes identified not just bourgeois ideology as a culprit but its junior partner, petit bourgeois ideology. Though analysed by Marx, the petit bourgeoisie was a relatively recent social class or sub-class, certainly in its new guise in 1950s France. It represented a relatively small social section, wedged between the capitalist (or fully bourgeois) class on the one hand, and the masses, the people or the working class on the other.

Shopkeepers, middle managers and the self-employed could all be considered members of the petit bourgeoisie; essentially, it was a class, in Barthes' Marxian conception, that copied the bourgeoisie's values without the material means to be a capitalist or a boss.

It was for this reason that Barthes considered petit bourgeois ideology as more pernicious in the fast-growing consumer culture of the 1950s: it put forward the key belief that social betterment – what we (laughingly) call today 'social mobility' – could come about through individual promotion, and not through collective struggle in trade unions, workplaces and the streets (as the 1930s had proven). Barthes implicitly connected this individualist project of finding a better life with self-delusion, brilliantly illustrated in *Mythologies* by the women's magazine aimed at those with modest household incomes, with privileged recipes for partridge that none of its readership would have the financial (or social) wherewithal to cook.[13] In other words, the most insidious aspect to myth was that it encouraged us, individually, to aspire. Aspiration – as opposed to the possibility or actuality of success – was a key element in self-delusion. The politics of the petit bourgeoisie is not necessarily reactionary – the Russian Marxist Leon Trotsky famously described the petit bourgeois as a 'weather-vane'. Indeed, in 1936 in France, many petit bourgeois people had supported the left-wing and progressive Popular Front government, even joining the strike and occupation movement (as opposed to the petit bourgeoisie in Germany who had largely capitulated to Hitler and the Nazis). But, by the 1950s, petit bourgeois politics had become largely reactionary, with its support for the xenophobia of Pierre Poujade's (short-lived) Union of Shopkeepers and Artisans' party, which (rather like the UK Independence Party today in Britain) made an electoral splash in 1956 on the back of a dislike of a centralized, ruling class and political elite whose imposition of high taxes was hitting the hard-working businesses and 'small' voiceless people who could not turn to trade unions or to collective struggle to defend themselves. As well as a danger of promoting a return to fascism (Barthes presciently pointed out in *Mythologies* that one of Poujade's more unsavoury colleagues, a parachutist in the French–Algerian war of 1954–62 who was proud of the French army's use of torture against the Algerian insurgents, was none other than the young French fascist Jean Marie Le Pen), petit bourgeois ideology also tended, in Barthes' view, to attract working-class people with its subtle ideas of self-promotion. This occurred especially at this time in the 1950s, when class struggle was at a low ebb as French capitalism began its thirty years of economic growth (1944–73) known as *Les Trente glorieuses*. Indeed, one of the other 'happy' myths that Barthes explored was the Parisian transport workers' strike in 1955, which, he suggested, had nothing to do with individualism and everything to do with collective action and the resultant social effects for all of society's classes.[14]

The consequent *embourgeoisement* – whereby the working masses seemingly began to identify with capitalism as the only system that could satisfy their social and personal needs – was a crucial element in the maintenance of the social status quo that the bourgeoisie needed in order to carry on its class rule and exploitation. In other words, the petit bourgeoisie was seen as a Trojan horse in left-wing, progressive politics, at a time in mid-1950s France when the Soviet Union was considered to be – especially after its invasion of Hungary in 1956 and the revelations, following Stalin's death in 1953, of the Gulag camps – as socially and politically bankrupt as Western capitalism. Petit bourgeois ideology 'worked' because it depoliticized phenomena at any moment, against which Barthes tried to mobilize radical acts of explanation (or repoliticization). If to explain why the world is the way that it is could be seen as an anti-petit bourgeois act, it was because petit bourgeois ideology could not stomach, argued Barthes, the disorder that such an explanation would certainly introduce: 'the world is all right, as long as we do not look too closely at it', seemed to be the petit bourgeois mantra.

It is at this moment of crisis in communist world politics that we see in France (and in Britain) the growth of a new left beyond the reach of Moscow-dominated politics. In 1956 Barthes was instrumental in the launch of a new left-wing journal with links across Western and Eastern Europe, called *Arguments*. With Edgar Morin, a former member of the French Communist Party, and with other intellectuals from Eastern Europe who had escaped the tyranny of the Soviet Bloc, Barthes played an important role, especially in the first two years of the journal's six-year history.

But there are two key elements of *Mythologies* we need to retain here. First, *Mythologies* was not a treatise on 1950s French politics; rather, it underlined the social nature of a pathology in Western capitalism, whereby, within each of our psychic dispositions, we convince and delude ourselves, at the very moments when we are not at our most politically astute. Barthes made this point neatly and subtly in relation to a front cover of *Paris Match* (the right-wing and petit bourgeois magazine) depicting a black boy saluting, which seemed, subliminally, to encourage public support for France's threatened empire during this difficult period of decolonization and anti-colonialism. He described encountering the photograph when, 'at the barber', he was 'offered' a copy (notice his passivity here) – in other words, when his political guard was at its lowest.[15] Indeed, the same inattention to the subject could be attributed to many of the other social phenomena analysed in *Mythologies*: drinking wine, buying washing powder, reading the agony aunts, going to the theatre or cinema, or watching advertisements. Barthes was implying that it is during our moments of leisure (of which there were significantly more in 1950s France, especially with the introduction of an eight-hour day, more available credit and paid holidays) that we are most susceptible to the ideological distortions of myth and of petit bourgeois ideology.

However, the second key element of *Mythologies* – and crucially for our aim in this book to show Barthes' life in his work – is that

Barthes was always speaking through 'himself': all of the self-delusions (and 'happy' myths) described in *Mythologies* (could quite easily be seen to) apply, first and foremost, if only theoretically, to Barthes the mythologist himself. In other words, within this social psychoanalysis of the French mind of the 1950s, there was a personal dimension. Barthes might describe 'bourgeois ideology' as an 'imposter' (a word Barthes would use of himself in the aftermath of 1968); he might be acutely aware of the bourgeoisie as 'discourse' in the Bayonne area of France in his youth (especially via his grandmother Berthe). But the critique of the bourgeoisie and its perfidious handmaiden, the petit bourgeoisie, could be seen as a vast *auto*-critique, part of an attempt to strike out elements of his own upbringing.

It is here then, in his most systematic critique of Western society's encouragement of self-delusion, that Barthes could be seen to be taking himself, somewhat selflessly, as a prime *subject* of self-delusions – albeit one who is able to step, eventually, outside and judge their harmfulness as a semiologist – turning himself (as it were) inside out. It was a strategy that was to be repeated in key texts published later in his career. The self as social experiment might come straight out of André Gide, but Gide was born forty years before Barthes, back in the mid-nineteenth century; Barthes' new self-as-social-experiment was one for the mass media age of the 1950s.

Nevertheless, as well as (or despite) the auto-critique played out in it, *Mythologies* made a number of key political, ideological and aesthetic points about modern society. *Mythologies* was not concerned with the 'commodity fetishism' that we might find exposed by the Situationists led by Guy Debord, nor with alienation as analysed by Henri Lefebvre; it was not objects that twisted our desires (our ideologies and actions did this): their role was one of providing warmth within alienation, of generating distortion as (misguided) social disalienation.[16]

Two other important points emerged from *Mythologies*. First, Barthes borrowed a central notion from his reading of Ferdinand de Saussure's work and its commentary by his friend Julien Greimas – namely, that nonsense (and/or 'non-sense') was still a form of meaning. Following Saussure's signifier/signified distinction, Barthes finessed his 'degree zero' theory of meaning to suggest that there was no degree zero – a space outside meaning – as all meanings can be continually hoisted into a new signifying chain indefinitely. In this first wave of Saussure's ideas in France (broadly speaking, the 1950s), Barthes underlined that language – like myth – was inexorably beholden to second-order meanings that distorted the original meaning. Furthermore, he insisted, humans were not actually able to look at all the different levels of meaning of an object simultaneously, and Barthes provides a good metaphor for this: while travelling in a car, try looking at the window and the country-side simultaneously.[17]

One critic has suggested that the 'young' Barthes ended with *Mythologies*, and the 'mature' Barthes started with 'Myth Today'. Indeed, Barthes' use of Saussure and semiology in the latter was markedly absent in any of his writings up until then, including the 51 short essays in *Mythologies*.[18] As well as marking a new era for the left intelligentsia (the New Left, the final end of Stalinism), 1956 was also the year when Barthes expressed his desire, in a letter to Rebeyrol, to become a *chercheur* (researcher), and no longer to be an intellectual. As we have said, Barthes struggled through the 1950s to secure employment, moving from one research post to another, via various smaller, short-term posts. It was following the publication of *Mythologies* in spring 1957 that Barthes began to edge nearer to a full-time career in research. He was, from 1 October 1955 to 15 September 1959, a lowly *attaché au cnrs pour la sociologie* (sociology attaché at the cnrs), which was followed by a short period (15 September 1959 to 30 March 1960) in which he was unemployed. Then, in 1960, he was given a full-time post at the new vith section of the École pratique des hautes études (EPHE), which Georges Friedmann had set up with Edgar Morin and Violette Morin (Barthes having already worked with Friedmann and Morin in 1955 and 1956 on the workplace clothing project).[19]

The highly original use of semiology in *Mythologies* led, in 1958, to discussions concerning clothing and fashion forms. Barthes' interest in fashion and in language put him in a unique position, just as he met the linguist André Martinet in 1959 (introduced by his old friends from Alexandria and Bucharest, the semiologist Julien Greimas and the stylistician Pierre Guiraud). Claude Lévi-Strauss declined to be involved but gave Barthes good advice on researching the written fashion item and on reading the classic work on the folktale by the Russian Formalist Vladimir Propp, *Morphology of the Folktale* (though it was only available in English until the French translation in 1970). Thus began a rather one-sided acquaintance in which Lévi-Strauss remained distant from Barthes, but Barthes was deeply influenced and respectful of the anthropologist. Barthes also discussed fashion and clothing with the phenomenologist philosopher Maurice Merleau-Ponty. Other thinkers that influenced Barthes as he moved towards structuralist approaches using semiology were the information logician Benoît Mandelbrot, the fashion theorist Alfred Kroeber and the linguist-phonologist Nicolas Trubetzkoy.

Barthes' work in the popular theatre – which continued until he took up his full-time research post in 1960 – had brought him into contact with various aspects of contemporary media, especially photography. As well as the fascinating commentary on Roger Pic's photographic record of the Berliner Ensemble's 1954 visit to Paris and the seminal production of Brecht's *Mother Courage*, he also analysed a wide set of photographic material in *Mythologies*: in addition to the black boy saluting on the front cover of *Paris Match*, he studied The Family of Man exhibition, a MOMA exhibition in New York that opened in Paris in 1956 containing photography used in elections and portraits of famous actors. This interest in photography – combined with his language-based research into clothing and fashion – led to his appointment in the 'sociology of media' that the vith section of the EPHE had set up. Even though Barthes would slowly distinguish his use of semiology from the discipline of sociology, it is perhaps too obvious to underline the deeply social way in which he approached all of his research projects: put simply, Barthes was interested in how humans make sense of, make intelligible, the modern world around them. If we combine this sensitivity to how we 'read' the world with the belief that 'writing' is the only way to resist accommodation to the distortions and injustices of Western society, Barthes would then go on to articulate – and eventually collapse – this writing/reading nexus across the turbulent years of the 1960s.

At this time, Barthes also met the great historian of myth Georges Dumézil, who played the role of Philippe Rebeyrol for Michel Foucault by helping to find him short-term teaching posts while Foucault wrote his PhD thesis between 1955 and 1959. Barthes' friendship with the latter, introduced by the mutual friend Robert Mauzi, lasted into the early 1960s. Although there were numerous interests and approaches that the two men held in common, one they did not share was their attitude to homosexuality: Barthes was as discreet as Foucault was exhibitionist. Barthes also met François Wahl in 1956, via the novelist Michel Butor, and Wahl was to become Barthes' editor at Les Éditions du seuil for the rest of his career. There were also important meetings with the Italian novelists Italo Calvino and Umberto Eco at this time, and Barthes began to make a series of research trips to Italy in the late 1950s (especially to Milan in 1958), not to mention visiting the United States in 1959, following which he wrote a brief piece on Bernard Buffet's painterly versions of New York. Wahl then became the partner of the Cuban-born writer Severo Sarduy, and they, with Barthes, began to travel regularly together to Morocco.

Interestingly, in 1959 Barthes tried to repeat the success of the monthly *Mythologies* with a new column in Nadeau's *Les Lettres nouvelles*, now a weekly magazine. The success was very limited, however, despite his stinging criticism of Malraux in *Tragédie et hauteur*, one of Barthes' last pieces on theatre, because he abruptly abandoned the popular theatre movement just as he was appointed to the EPHE.[20] Barthes had thus assembled a rich array of new and radical thinkers: from Brecht, the Marx of *The German Ideology* (which was only recently available in the 1950s), Sartre and his commitment, Adamov and his theatre, and Lévi-Strauss and his radical structuralist anthropology, to the more ambiguous names of Saussure, Michelet and Robbe-Grillet.

As well as being a key year in his career, 1960 was also the height of the brutal Algerian war of independence waged against France's empire. Though his friend Bernard Dort signed the famous '121' petition in favour of the right of French soldiers to desert the war (set up by Nadeau and Maurice Blanchot), Barthes signed an alternative, less militant petition (with Morin and others) calling for a negotiated settlement recognizing Algeria's right to self-determination. Indeed, though Barthes was clearly aligned with the radical, Marxist (but non-Stalinist) left in the 1950s, his attitude to militant activity – beyond his agitating one in the popular theatre movement – was one of passivity, due to his aversion to the 'hysteria' of leftist political discourse, preferring the 'calm' of the biting intellectual critique of writing, the political cut-and-thrust of essayistic debate, and the corrosive power of irony best conveyed by the literary essay and now to be found outside of the theatre. One of Barthes' most forthright statements of his essayistic politics occurred precisely in 1960, in his essay in *Arguments*, 'Écrivains et écrivants' (Authors and Writers), which is perhaps the best definition of his essayism; other essays around this time were stunning for the richness and rhetorical finesse, as well as thought- and research-provoking ideas – I choose my own favourites here:

'The Witch' (1959); 'From Gemstones to Jewellery' (1962); 'The Eiffel Tower' (1964); 'Rhetoric of the Image' (1964); 'The Plates of the *Encyclopedia*' (1964).[21] These pieces showed – among the many other prefaces, commentaries and book reviews that we might group under 'essayism' – what Edgar Morin had presciently said at the end of the last number of *Arguments* in 1962, while explaining why the various intellectuals running the journal were now going their own way: Barthes, for his part, suggested Morin was now keen to look after his own oeuvre.

4

From Semiology to Structuralism

Now financially secure in 1960, Barthes sold the summer house he had inherited from Noémi Révelin; with Hendaye becoming too touristy, Barthes and his mother bought a small house called La Maison carboué inland, in Urt, a small town on the left bank of the Adour, near Bayonne. However, typical of Barthes' turbulent and unpredictable life, he still had no career in 1959. He had once again lost his grant from the CNRS; he was also preparing to leave behind the popular theatre movement and the journal *Théâtre populaire*. Furthermore, he was no longer friends with Dort, nor with the playwright Michel Vinaver with whom he had struck up a friendship. (Vinaver – touted as France's Brecht – regretted losing Barthes as a key reader of his theatrical work.) Distance had also opened up between Barthes and his very first literary mentor, Maurice Nadeau. Yet, in 1960, as we have seen, he landed a post in the newly created VIth section of the École pratique des hautes études (EPHE), with Friedmann, Edgar Morin and Violette Morin and under the leadership of the medieval historian Jacques Le Goff. By 1962, despite not having a doctorate, he had become a *directeur d'études* (research director) in the 'sociology of signs, symbols and representations' at the EPHE, where he would research and teach until 1977.

At the same time, Barthes was beginning to garner influence in a wide number of academic, intellectual and even political arenas. One need only read the 1962 essay on Brecht by Communist Party dissident Louis Althusser to see this.[1] Does this mean that

Barthes was no longer 'marginal'? In her recent biography, Marie Gil argues that the end of his marginalization did not occur until after May 1968; before this, Barthes would, as we shall see, have some bruising and concerted attacks on his work from establishment academics such as Raymond Picard. Indeed, in 1963, Barthes' collection of essays *On Racine* – some of which were written just as he became disillusioned with the popular theatre movement in 1959, for which the domination of drama and literary culture by Racine's theatre, especially in French schools, was doubtless partly to blame – began to generate attacks from the conservative wing of literary criticism, notably in the form of the Sorbonne's Racine specialist Raymond Picard. Picard, we will remember, had been a contemporary of Barthes and Rebeyrol in their late adolescence, and, unlike Barthes, had benefited from an education in literature at the *grande école* in Paris, the Ecole normale supérieure (ENS). In the rather ugly ganging-up on Barthes, who was deemed to be the spokesperson of the *nouvelle critique* emerging out of structuralist (not to mention Freudian, existentialist, phenomenological and Marxian) approaches to analysing literature, it was the young journal *Tel Quel* that was to play a key supporting role to Barthes while he was largely pilloried in the press, with little other support.

Nevertheless, with his prolific writing of essays, his widely read *Mythologies* and now a post at the EPHE, Barthes was beginning to be noticed outside narrow left-wing intellectual circles. Indeed, the early 1960s saw various agencies looking him up for his incisive ideas on social communication. In 1963 Georges Péninou – whom Barthes had met in the sanatorium in Saint-Hilaire-du-Touvet twenty years before – signed up for one of his seminars and, as a marketing specialist for *Publicis*, revealed Barthes' semiology to the advertising world. Barthes also gave a lecture to Renault on the mythology of the car, which possibly implied that even *Mythologies* had been, in some sense, 'recuperated' by the very marketing of objects it sought to expose.[2]

The writing on sport in *Mythologies* and its relationship to popular culture, specifically the first chapter on wrestling, led to an invitation to work on a one-hour documentary, *What is Sport?*, by the Franco-Canadian writer Hubert Aquin (and published post-humously in 2004 as a book called *Le sport et les hommes*), for which Barthes provided the written accompaniment to the film once it had been made. Broadcast on Canadian television in June 1961, the documentary film went on to win Le Prix de la réalisation at the film festival at Cortina d'Ampezzo in Italy in 1962. Contacted by Aquin in April 1960, Barthes spent ten days in January 1961 working with him in Montreal, also lecturing at the universities of Laval and Montreal. Though Barthes was unable to write a commentary for a film in which any changes were possible, he had been involved at an earlier stage of the process in the selection of themes, images and sports to be covered. Indeed, the whole process was a good example of Barthes' experience of text-image work, which he had already begun with photography, in relation to Roger Pic's record of the Berliner Ensemble performances in Paris in the 1950s. But now, in 1960, he was working on moving images, while also writing his first pieces on film theory and semiotics.[3]

What is Sport? emphasized, as both film and text, the phenomenological and poetic aspects to various sports (cycling, bull-fighting, motor-racing, ice hockey and football). His theoretical interest in cinema subsequently came across in the approach that he adopted in the written commentary in the documentary, whereby sport is represented as *filmed* spectacle (framed, if you like), rather than as an unmediated event – hence the inclusion of images of spectators too (and not dissimilar to Barthes' attention to the audience in his 1952 piece on wrestling). In other words, Barthes' commentary insisted on the social, lived experience of sport for the player and the spectators, rather than on any direct study of sport's physicality.[4]

This commission to work on the sport documentary was typical of Barthes' burgeoning career in the early 1960s, where consultancies were growing on the strength of his sociological and semiological writings.[5] In this period Barthes was also developing an interest in psychoanalysis, on Freud especially: first, via the work of his friend, the Germanist Marthe Robert, whose book on Franz Kafka was very favourably reviewed by Barthes in 1960; and second, through the psychoanalyst André Green, who had been enthused by *Mythologies*.[6] Both Green and Robert gave papers in Barthes' seminars at the EPHE in the early 1960s, as did a young Gérard Genette, a former Communist Party member and then briefly an activist in the Socialisme et barbarie group set up by Jean-François Lyotard, Claude Lefort and Cornelius Castoriadis.[7] The EPHE seminar thus became a space in which Barthes could try out his eclectic mix of theories and research approaches. After a period of work on myths and symbols, Barthes' seminars at the EPHE moved into two key areas: his seminar began as a programme of research on the semiology of food, clothing and shelter, using materials usually found in the national press, both daily and weekly; he then not unrelatedly launched, with Greimas, Violette Morin and the Franco-Bulgarian literary theorist Tzvetan Todorov, a study of narrative, both of its functions and of its anthropological significance in modern societies, importantly introducing Roman Jakobson's work on language and poetry in a moment of neo-formalist exploration. All of these research projects revolved around a new journal emerging from the EPHE and its mass culture research centre.

Launched by Morin, Friedman and Barthes in 1961, *Communications* was the in-house journal of C.E.C.MAS, the Centre for the Study of Mass Culture. It is here that we see Barthes beginning to recreate the 'Alpine Oxford' of his time in the sanatorium – his 'undergraduate' training in Saint-Hilaire-du-Touvet, if you like, followed by his 'postgraduate' training in Leysin involving reading Michelet and long discussions with Fournié on (Trotskyist) Marxism. Indeed, during and following May 1968, the EPHE was to become a crucial site of ideological opposition for Barthes, especially, as we shall see, in the 1968–9 seminars on Balzac's story 'Sarrasine'. As a relatively independent research grouping, the EPHE was able to do things that no other academic and research institution could, often involving researchers with two posts, one at a university and the other in the EPHE. But this double appointment did not apply to Barthes, whose material circumstances – the luck, one might say, of living with his mother – did not now require him to accumulate academic posts as supplementary sources of income. Viewed another way, living with his mother (including the inheritance from Noémi, his maternal grandmother) freed Barthes from needing to have a 'full' academic career, and he could devote his time to his EPHE seminar – hence his commentary on the EPHE as a rare institution in which one (he) could be happy.[8]

This narrow concentration of his working life within the EPHE also allowed him the 'luxury' of continuing to work with other intellectual journals. Involved in the 1956 launch of the new-left journal *Arguments* (owned by former Resistance network and *nouveau roman* publisher, Éditions de Minuit), Barthes served for two periods on its editorial board: from 1956 to 1957, with Jean Duvignaud, a sociologist colleague from his time at *Théâtre populaire*, and Edgar Morin as director; and then from 1961 to 1962. Apart from the historical significance of this journal and the intellectual influence that it had on the European Left at the start of the 1960s, it was its dissolution that was the most telling for Barthes' career. In the very last number of *Arguments* (in 1962), Morin, the journal's director, explained the 'auto-dissolution' that the committee had decided to implement: the end of *Arguments* was, he wrote in the valedictory comments, due to a diaspora – the people running it were going elsewhere to do other things (for example, Duvignaud to Tunisia), and Barthes, wrote Morin, was 'more and more oriented towards his own *oeuvre*'.[9] This was graphically illustrated in the book advertisements at the end of this final number of *Arguments*, where we see Bruce Morrissette's book on the *nouveaux romans* of Alain Robbe-Grillet being advertised alongside the name of the person who wrote the book's preface, Roland Barthes.[10] The dissolution of *Arguments* in the early 1960s was happening, therefore, as Barthes' own oeuvre started to become important in itself, and not just as a vehicle for new theories such as semiology or structuralism. This is not to say that Barthes then abandoned his theoretical activities as his own writing began to take precedence. On the contrary, he was also working hard in academic research in this period of the early 1960s; and we will see how these two distinct activities – teaching and writing – were to become more and more permeable, as he operated them in tandem.

A good example of Barthes looking after his own writer's oeuvre came, appropriately enough, in the essay published in *Arguments* in 1960, 'Authors and Writers', a programmatic piece which, according to some critics, seemed to signal Barthes' political 'disengagement'.[11] Above all, this essay, as a subtle self-inscription, was a great Montaignean moment for Barthes' writing. No longer, it implied, was literature a radical set of questions posed to the world (something he had already established in 1952 with the literary questionnaire produced with Nadeau); rather, the Author (as opposed to the 'Writer') – of fiction, but also of the essay especially (Barthes really is bending the stick here) – 'is always an inductor of ambiguities', and is only ever about (more) writing.

Furthermore, his essay argued, the true responsibility of the Author is to shoulder the fact that literature is an *engagement manqué* (failed political commitment). This *in*transitivity of the writer (not surprising perhaps for novelists in this *nouveau roman* world) now also applied to all writers – that is, in his case, the essayist. The *écrivain* is now merely a conduit through which language operates: 'for language is precisely that structure whose very goal . . . is to neutralize the true and the false'.[12] As the title of his 1966 paper 'To Write: An Intransitive Verb?' implied, essay as fiction – or rather the 'essayistic', the genre inaugurated by Montaigne – was now the central concern for Barthesian aesthetics.[13] One cannot help feeling that, now that he had a fixed job, Barthes' critical practice of prefaces, book reviews and commentaries, which had supported him (materially, intellectually and politically) through the lean years of 1946–59, could now benefit from the 'luxury' of denying his writing any 'object' other than language, writing and literature itself. This was (to pick up on his 'degree zero' thesis from 1953) a crucial Orphean moment in Barthes' essayism: the more he looked at (after) his own literary essayism, the more it slipped away (into language), and the more the (writing) self could become dissolved across this 'linguistic turn' (of which fashion was the perfect example because, although agentless, it still, paradoxically, relied on human input). But – and this is crucial for our presentation of Barthes as a social writer – the essay 'Authors and Writers' ended with the following suggestive comment: 'language is this paradox: the institutionalization of subjectivity.'[14] In other words, to communicate was to be both subject and object of an institution, to be both an individual self and a social human, at one and the same time.

It was at exactly the same time as Barthes began to 'look after' his own literary oeuvre that we see his growing interest in semiology and structuralism. Echoing the title of André Martinet's treatise on linguistics – *Eléments de linguistique générale* (Elements of General Linguistics), published in 1960 – Barthes produced his first fully theoretical study of semiology. *Elements of Semiology* was more an essay than an article (it first appeared in *Communications* in 1964); this was quickly recognized when it was republished in 1965 alongside the Denoël/Gonthier edition of *Writing Degree Zero*. *Elements of Semiology* displayed what was now a Barthesian trademark of using examples from daily life, combined with a highly erudite explanation of Saussure's semiology. If – as in 'Myth Today' – Barthes was at the barber when he encountered the image of the black boy saluting on the front cover of *Paris Match*, his examples of semiology's understanding of communication in *Elements of Semiology* seven years later involved a panoply of banal social objects: the Highway Code for road users, the colours of the traffic light, fashion as 'written' or as photographed, cars, furniture, architecture and food.

The Saussure-inspired reading of everyday life was, typically, combined with an erudite use of ancient Greek and an engagement with the philosophy of Merleau-Ponty (one of the first thinkers to take Saussure seriously), not to mention Hegel, Gilles-Gaston Granger and C. S. Peirce. In addition, Barthes happily ranged across German, English and even Danish and Chinese in the examples he supplied. But Barthes' main aim in *Elements of Semiology* was to show that all interpretation of phenomena in human society passes, in some way, through language (in both the narrower linguistic and the wider communicative senses of the word). Indeed, in *Elements of*

The famous Citroën DS car analysed by Barthes in *Mythologies* in 1957.

Semiology, Barthes made the structuralist move of radically amending Saussure's view of the relationship of linguistics to semiology. Using the linguistic theories of Louis Hjelmslev and Jakobson – not to mention the semantic work carried out by Émile Benveniste – Barthes took the important step of inverting Saussure's claim that linguistics was merely a branch of a wider system of semiology.[15] Barthes used the *langue/parole* (language/speech) distinction made by Saussure to show that *langue*, as a 'system of contractual values' that resists the modifications coming from a single individual, was consequently 'a *social* institution'.[16] In other words – and this seems to summarize well Barthes' own investment in 'language' – communication ('language' in the widest sense) rested, according to *Elements of Semiology*, on a Hegelian, social dialectic whereby humans, when they communicate, draw on a socially defined lexicon, but which, though it may seem to the person communicating to be to the contrary, is actually unaffected as a system by that (and each) person's utterance(s). As with clothing and the changes in fashion over time and history, language does indeed change, but imperceptibly; humans, collectively, shape and change language across time, without there being any easily identifiable human agency that does this (what sociolinguists call the problem of 'actuation').

We have indeed moved on from the introduction to *Writing Degree Zero*, in which Hébert's use of bawdy language during the French Revolution seemed to be mobilized as an example of how a change in language is signalled. And yet, as we saw, such a change was vastly exaggerated given the imposed, bourgeois nature of French between 1650 and 1850. In 1964 Barthes was applying a similar form of scepticism to human individual agency in relation to the social, but now it was to a much wider category than simply writing or literature (as the 'degree zero' thesis had done); in *Elements of Semiology*, Barthes was arguing that the semiological – the idea that communication is based on a differential system of meanings – was part of a wider notion in which language operated as the foundation of human experience in its social totality.

Part of this move towards structuralism, towards seeing language as the basis of human interaction and social experience, was dependent on Barthes' growing interest in psychoanalysis. Thus *Elements of Semiology* provided brief but significant discussions of Jacques Lacan's work, and especially of the idea that the psyche, the unconscious, operates 'differentially', as if it, too, were a language. Using Lacan alongside Jung, Freud and Lévi-Strauss, Barthes' social psychoanalysis began to build on his work in *Mythologies*; and *Elements of Semiology* continued to operate the investment of himself in his research. Though the examples in *Elements of Semiology* were drawn from the daily, and contemporary, social life of 1960s France, Barthes hesitated to interpose his own subjective experience. Or, rather, the whole of *Elements of Semiology* was concerned with the subjective experience of language and communication, for which Barthes no longer needed to mention going to the barber and being handed a copy of *Paris Match*. In this sense, Barthes had imbibed Merleau-Ponty's phenomeno-logical account of experiencing difference within language and communication.

There is another reason for which we might consider the Barthes of 1965 as distinct from the Barthes of *Mythologies* ten years before, and that is what he called, looking back in the 1970s, the 'dream of scientificity' in his 1960s work. As with all Barthesian statements, especially those reflecting on himself, we need to be provisional in our interpretation of them, and we will see this provisionality in a moment. However, it is undeniable that, alongside his highly involved study of fashion and language during the period 1957–67, Barthes developed, if only briefly (provisionally), a scientific method for analysing culture in all of its manifestations. *Elements of Semiology* confirmed this; it was the first in a series of classifications, or super-classifications, that – followed by 'The Introduction to Structural Analysis of Narratives', his seminar work on rhetoric and then by *The Fashion System* – used taxonomy and scientific classification systems to analyse how meanings were generated in social situations.[17] However, as we shall see, these super-classifications in the mid 1960s that used Saussurean semiology and structuralism to show how identity – in all senses – was differential would soon need to be reined in because, as Barthes discovered, the formalism they employed was highly formulaic: a true formalism needed to allow the literary text not to be lost in the rush to systematize its ways of generating meanings. Essentially then, by the time Barthes published *s/z* in 1970, his analysis was to have shifted, and it was not simply May '68 that encouraged this 'shift', but his realization of the stark limitations of *over*-classifying.

Published in *Communications* in 1965 as a preface to the special number coordinated by Barthes, 'Introduction to the Structural Analysis of Narratives' was perhaps Barthes' most systematic, if only programmatic, advocacy of a methodology.[18] Using Vladimir Propp's classic study *Morphology of the Folktale*, which was suggested by Lévi-Strauss and read in English, Barthes' introduction to the functional analyses performed by Todorov, Greimas, Genette, Violette Morin, Claude Bremond, Umberto Eco and Christian Metz that followed in *Communications* – on James Bond, *Dangerous Liaisons*, film narrative, funny stories in the press and mythical narratives – set out the general aim of structural analyses of narratives. These aims were to show that we, as social humans, are (in some sense) determined by the stories we read and tell, and that, overall, the (seemingly infinite) number of stories across the world and across human history are actually reducible to a very small number of possible models – seven in total. In this sense, the project was extraordinarily reductive, allowing a rather formalistic anthropology to contain – that is, limit – the complexities of human exchange. But for Barthes, it was ideal.

If we remember that Marie Gil has characterized Barthes as an 'oscillator', then this 'scientific' attempt to describe, globally, the functions and models of narratives serves as a good example. In good Houdini style, Barthes' structural theories of narrative set up a tight and authoritative method with which to analyse how narratives worked, only for him to spend the next ten years or so undermining (or deconstructing) this very approach. At exactly the same time as the project on the structural analysis of narratives (1964–5) and the publication of *Elements of Semiology* (which was also programmatic, if not schematic and systematic) – not to mention a rather dry account of fashion clothing and language (finally published in 1967 as *The Fashion System*) – Barthes wrote a preface to the first collection of his essays, called *Critical Essays* (1964).

This introduction to a range of his essays from the 1950s was a significant attempt to show that the critic – who at this stage of Barthes' career was being differentiated from the academic – should be considered on a par with any writer, in that the critic is unable to say that he has the 'last word' on a text. Therefore, the critic, argued Barthes (on the very first page of the preface), 'is a writer'. It is not, he insists, that any 'style' or 'vision' should be appended to the critic's way of writing (as one might with a writer 'proper', such as a novelist or poet), but simply that the critic should have the right to talk obliquely – using *une parole indirecte* (indirect speech) – about the text in question.[19] This was to become an important moment for Barthes as a writer. He could continue to work at the EPHE with his structuralist colleagues on exposing how narratives work, but another, more powerful intellectual world – in this era of mass media – was beginning to open up a space for the 'critic' (be it of literature, film or any 'text'). And, of course, as a one-time popular theatre activist, Barthes' experience as a critic in the 1950s, especially for *Théâtre populaire*, gave him a head start in the 1960s.

Moreover, Brecht's epic theatre – central to a good number of the essays in the *Critical Essays* collection – is a critical theatre, a theatre that does not flatter its audience. Instead it positions them in such a way so as to be 'distanced' and therefore critical, 'oblique' even, in relation to the narrative on the stage. Applying Brecht's epic theatre to the writing of his essays is the nub of Barthes' essayism: the essay was, after all, a creative act, a piece of literature that was 'parametric' with the text being criticized, he suggested.[20] This notion of parametrism, which emerged from structuralism but also from Edgar Morin's sociological work, was both a guide and a limit, as well as (typically for Barthes) a way out, a step towards creating a new 'artistic text'. In other words, by 1964 Barthes had begun to cross an important line: a critic was no longer someone who receives (and then explains) a story. Rather, the critic was a writer who acted back upon the text. By 1968 Barthes was arguing that the critic 'rewrites',

Barthes in 1964.

're-covers', the text in question; the Author, as Barthes would famously claim in 1967, is now, to all intents and purposes, 'dead'.

In order to appreciate the line that Barthes crossed in this first half of the 1960s, one need only compare Barthes' criticism on Racine's theatre, written between 1959 and 1963 and collected in *On Racine*, with Lucien Goldmann's Marxist reading of Racine from the same time.[21] In *On Racine*, even though Barthes' studies of Racine's theatre were highly indebted to the newfangled Marxist and structuralist, as well as sociological, phenomenological and psychoanalytical, elements of *la nouvelle critique* – and for which Barthes was sternly rebuked by French academia and the mainstream press in the so-called 'Picard affair' – Barthes was already trying to move away from, or at least relativize, the 'scientific' results of *la nouvelle critique*. In one fell swoop, in the debate over 'History or Literature?', Barthes distanced himself subtly and carefully from the 'historicist' critic.[22] In the end, Marxism, sociologism, phenomenology, psychoanalysis and even structuralism all seemed to overlook one crucial element of 'text', specifically of literary texts. This element was literariness, or the text's innovative and particular use of language. The danger was that *la nouvelle critique* – in all its excitement about finally being able to bring Freud, Marx and Nietzsche to bear on literature – tended to 'miss' the text in question by 'naturalizing' it into another language (historical-materialist, sociological, experiential, unconscious and so on). Barthes' essayistic, parametric approach was not only 'oblique' (as we saw above), but (potentially) 'on a par' with the text in question.

So began a period in Barthes' writing that we might want to call 'creative criticism', whereby (as the name implies) the act of criticism of a text was itself a creative continuation of that text. And if literature was a question to the world, not an answer – as many of the essays in *Critical Essays* argue, in relation to Kafka, Butor, Robbe-Grillet, Queneau, Yves Velan and even Michelet – then literary and other forms of textual criticism should be a question too. This 'oblique' but parametric approach to text was precisely the platform on which Barthes was to defend modern criticism in his essay *Criticism and Truth* (1966), against the *belle lettriste* scientism of Sorbonne literary criticism typified by Raymond Picard.

As noted in Chapter One, it was not only Philippe Rebeyrol, Barthes' childhood best friend, who managed to achieve, academically, what illness prevented Barthes from doing. Raymond Picard had been selected for the *hypokhâgne* back in 1936 and, by 1965, was a successful, if rather traditional, professor at the Sorbonne and a specialist of that national treasure, the classical playwright Jean Racine. Having read Barthes' *On Racine* and various other critics who claimed to be part of *la nouvelle critique* in the 1960s, Picard wrote an essay accusing these new critics of being 'imposters'.[23] Barthes claimed, in an interview that replied to Picard's broadside against *la nouvelle critique*, that his reading of Racine had opened up a much wider question of how to relate to classical writers in the twentieth century and that his reading was about 'infidelity', a theme very relevant to 1960s France; he even claimed thereby to be the true guardian of French values, a somewhat ironic claim glibly used by the interviewer as the title of the interview.[24] However, much of *On Racine* – despite its intellectual effect on *la querelle* (as the public quarrel with Picard is now known) – is seen by Marie Gil to be about Barthes' own psychic binaries.

In her biography of Barthes, Gil suggests that Barthes could see the 'tragedy' at work in Racine's theatre, for the simple reason that, without a father, his family relations were themselves distorted.[25] But this is a purely personal reading of Barthes' writing, one that ignores the social dimensions and pretensions of his work. It is, nevertheless, necessary to point out that Barthes felt exposed, surrounded in the 'affaire Picard' – even Lévi-Strauss did not really support him, and Jean-Paul Weber's retort to Picard (in the same series as Picard's essay, published by Jean-Jacques Pauvert) only went so far as to defend Weber's own version of thematic criticism.[26] Indeed, the scientism and lack of structuralism in Weber's thematic criticism was doubtless now anathema to Barthes, who was moving, as we suggested, towards a wholly creative form of criticism, far from the 'rigorous objectivity' and 'scientific doctrine' vaunted by Weber's defence of thematic criticism.

This fundamental difference from Weber made *Criticism and Truth* all the more poignant because one of its key aims was to show that criticism, far from being a personal opinion on a text, was, in fact – just like a literary text – a social form that connects communities in cohesive and antagonistic ways, almost to the point that literary criticism should be viewed (as Barthes suggested with narratives the year before) as a global, human phenomenon, and possibly as having more models available than the object that it purported to 'explain' (that is, narrative with only seven archetypes or models, according to Propp's *Morphology of the Folktale*).

Written in February 1966, *Criticism and Truth* underlined the social nature of the critic, found in the multi-authored culture of the medieval period in which writing had been a social (rather than an individual) act involving a *scriptor*, *commentator*, *auctor* and *compilator*.[27] Barthes was also fully aware of the 'solitude of the act of criticism', but it nevertheless brought the critic and the writer together, in a social way, now both faced with exactly the same object (a social one if ever there was one): language. Indeed, it is easy to underestimate the pivotal nature of *Criticism and Truth* not only for Barthes' career and writing, but for its social pretensions: 'to write is not to enter into an easy relationship with an *average* of all possible readers, it is to enter into a difficult relationship with our own language.'[28]

Though this emphasis on language seemed to be discounting the faceless, amorphous 'public' that a writer (be they critic or writer 'proper') normally considers when writing – in a seemingly *a*social moment – the injunction by Barthes here, that it was to a writer's own language that he must pay attention, was at once actually *more* social. Language as a profoundly human communicative phenomenon – in the Bakhtinian sense that Barthes would soon discover when he began to work with Julia Kristeva – was far more 'social' than the writer who spent all his energy wondering what a general ('average') but individually non-existent reader might do. Indeed, one could go further and suggest that the writer caring most about his language was taking a democratic, as well as a social, approach to the readers in that he could also add his own language. Thus the (potentially infinite) circulation of written language must be preferred to the 'closure' of an imagined (illusory) reader: 'to write', declared Barthes, 'is *already* to think (to learn a language is to learn how one thinks in that language)'. In a parallel interview in the *Figaro littéraire*, in an extended reply to Picard, Barthes went further:

> modern criticism has the merit of using the same language
> as the literature of our time. A modern novel has, more
> or less clearly, a Marxist or psychoanalytical background.
> That language is familiar to modern criticism.[29]

Following this interview, Barthes made the first of his trips to Japan, happy, it would seem, to leave a France that was (erroneously) taking him to be the typical exponent of *la nouvelle critique*; he had, however, already left this behind by 1964, in search of a 'creative' form of criticism. We will look at this creative criticism in the next chapter, but we must first consider the other effect of his theatre work.

It is quite clear that as Barthes abandoned the popular theatre movement in 1960, it was his work on photography that benefited. The year 1964 saw the publication of his work with photographer André Martin on the photo-text called 'The Eiffel Tower', a brilliant commentary by Barthes alongside Martin's intricate images.[30] Not only did Barthes analyse the tower semiologically, structurally, he hinted at its writerly status, especially in the opening canard, where he stated that Guy de Maupassant disliked the Tower so intensely that he ate regularly in its top-floor restaurant, as this was the only place where he could not see it!

The key meeting for Barthes in this first half of the 1960s – with Catholic novelist Philippe Sollers – would go on to define his social and intellectual milieu for the rest of his life and career. Though he never joined the editorial board of the journal *Tel Quel*, Barthes was its best-known fellow traveller. Launched by Sollers and backed by Jean Cayrol and Les Éditions du seuil, *Tel Quel* is probably the most influential French post-war journal, alongside Sartre's *Les Temps modernes*, at a time (1945–75) that we might call the *Trente glorieuses* of the intellectual publication in French. The poet Francis Ponge was the link that facilitated Barthes and Sollers' first meeting. However, Barthes' first encounter with *Tel Quel*, in a response to a question-naire in 1961, was surprisingly negative. Here, Barthes implied that *Tel Quel* (at least in 1961) was wrong to have an *inengagement* (lack of political commitment); though this might well be the 'truth' of literature, he opined, it could not be a 'general rule of behaviour' for a journal.[31] Published in *Critical Essays*, this interview might sit awkwardly next to 'Authors and Writers', which we suggested marks a step back from, if not redefines, his own essayistic 'engagement' – or perhaps Barthes was saying that *Tel Quel*'s members were merely 'Writers' not 'Authors'. Indeed, in 'Author and Writers', Barthes had suggested, but discounted, a third (degree zero?) possibility: that of the Author-Writer, a bastardized version that we should not overlook. Interestingly, if the discussion over political commitment prefigured the 'engagement' that *Tel Quel* would go on to develop after 1967 (following a brief *rapprochement* with French Communist Party intellectuals and especially during its Maoist phase of the early 1970s), Barthes offered here a tantalizing view of *his* future development in the 1970s (and already theorized in his 1956 article on playwright Michel Vinaver): 'tel quelism' – 'suspension of judge-ment', as he defined it – might be a way forward for the journal. But this came at a price, Barthes was suggesting. Given that it was not at all 'innocent', 'suspension' of judgement could be achieved only if it considered the day-to-day realities – what Barthes called 'this very fragile and obscure moment where the relation of a real event is going to be understood in its literary meaning'.[32] It was then a fundamentally *literary* approach to real-world events that Barthes seemed to be advocating to *Tel Quel*.

It is not surprising that *Tel Quel* would be open to the modernization of literature and criticism proposed by Barthes, given its support for the *nouveau roman*. Tactical and friendship-led, Barthes' association with *Tel Quel*, and especially with Sollers, could not hide the enormous contextual importance of this association. Just as *Tel Quel* was beginning to assimilate the 'structural revolution' taking place in mid-1960s France into its literary theory and practice, Barthes was becoming the leading literary theorist on the importance of structuralist linguistics – how it influenced the literary critic and literary criticism overall. Barthes' sympathy and advice for the young *Tel Quel* editorial team in 1961 was from someone who had also worked on journals in the 1950s. Indeed, as his influence grew in the mid-1960s, Barthes was invited onto the editorial boards of a number of other important journals, such as *Gulliver*, with Maurice Blanchot, in 1963, which never saw the light of day. Also in 1963 Barthes, Foucault and the poet Michel Deguy were invited onto the editorial committee of the prestigious journal *Critique*, whose new director, Jean Piel, was recruiting a new set of critics following the death of its founder Georges Bataille. Ironically, this was the moment when Barthes and Foucault, having been friends since 1955 – and Barthes having generously reviewed Foucault's first book, *Folie et déraison* (Madness and Civilization), in *Critique* in 1961 – became markedly distant in their relations, possibly over Sollers or the arrival on the scene of Foucault's future lifelong partner, Daniel Defert.[33]

Barthes was also, from 1961 to 1967, making links abroad. During a short visit to Morocco in 1965, he met the dean of the new Mohammed v University in Rabat, Zaghloul Morsy, who subsequently invited him to come and teach there in 1969. He also began to make regular visits to Japan (in May–June 1966, March–April 1967 and December 1967–January 1968), following an invitation from Maurice Pinguet, director of the Maison française in Tokyo. Pinguet would describe Barthes' Japan as like Stendhal's Italy – a utopia, as somewhere to live, with Barthes as the new Robinson Crusoe, deaf, it would seem, to the language of the society he had to come to visit.

5

May '68

The period from 1957 to 1971 saw Barthes in his theoretically most productive period. Drawing on his experiences in popular theatre, he had begun to develop his literary criticism into a more scientific approach, and semiological, structuralist and then post-structuralist analyses followed across the 1960s. His structuralist readings of Racinian theatre (*On Racine*, 1963) had drawn Barthes into a literary spat with the arch-conservative Sorbonne professor Raymond Picard. His *Critical Essays* (1964) showed both the politically engaged Brechtian and the polemical literary critic; *Elements of Semiology* (1964), the skilful semiotician; and *Criticism and Truth* (1966), the literary jouster. The academic post and financial stability of the appointment in 1960 encouraged Barthes, finally, to complete his doctoral thesis, which was published as *The Fashion System* (1967). It also allowed him to develop other areas of his 'structuralist activity' that had begun in *Mythologies*, especially in visual culture. A number of key essays on photography appeared in the EPHE in-house journal, *Communications*, between 1961 and 1964. Barthes also masterminded a special number of this journal, in 1966, on the 'structuralist analysis of narratives', which combined older, Russian-formalist theories of narrative with recent developments in Lévi-Strauss's structuralist anthropology to arrive at a 'functional' model of storytelling. The 'triumph' of structuralism in mid-1960s France was, however, to become anathema to a fast-moving political situation in the country.

'It is no longer the government that is being called into question, nor our institutions, not even France', declared France's prime minister Georges Pompidou, speaking to the Assemblée nationale on 14 May 1968 (following nearly two weeks of students' and then workers' uprisings); 'it is our very civilization.' Within two years of this sombre statement, Barthes would declare in an interview in 1970, 'The battle to crack open the West's symbolic order has begun.'[1] Between these two pronouncements – similar in their perception of May '68's assault on Western civilization – France went through the biggest general strike in human history (for the time) and watched helplessly as its young people started to challenge the very structure and ideological supports of French capitalism. Marie Gil sees May '68 as crucial for Barthes because he was, suddenly, no longer the marginalized intellectual and was obliged to find a new form of writing.[2]

Though Barthes had participated in a key movement in France in February – the defence of Henri Langlois, head of the controversial Cinémathèque in Paris, who had been summarily sacked by culture minister André Malraux in February 1968 (now seen as a harbinger of the May '68 *événements*) – he could still announce in a review of Sollers' two recent novels, *Logiques* and *Nombres* (both Paris, 1968), for the weekly magazine *Nouvel observateur* on the 30 April 1968 (three days before the start of the students' revolt) that 'the idea of revolution is dead in the West'.[3] And though he was not alone in misreading the seething social situation in France in early 1968, Barthes did seem to have been overtaken – overwhelmed even – by the events in France in the hot May of 1968. In future years, Barthes would look back on the whole experience as the major 'break', which, in the decadent early 1970s, he called the 'Mutation' or 'Shift' in society. This 'Mutation' seemed to refer as much to Barthes himself – especially to the shift between the 'Introduction to the Structural Analysis of Narratives' and *s/z* (that is, between 1965 and 1969) – as it did to French society in general.[4] But, at the time,

Barthes was one of the many intellectuals – 'mandarins' – who were roundly criticized by the ultra-left students leading the occupations, sit-ins, demonstrations and interminable 'general meetings'. Jean-Paul Sartre was one of the precious few intellectuals not considered 'recuperated' by the system. Structuralists and semiologists such as Barthes were considered to be apologists for the structured capitalist system that the students were violently rejecting: 'Structuralists do not come out onto the streets', goaded one piece of graffiti.[5]

Indeed, in a short but revealing article in the national press, in part about Barthes and his fellow colleague at the EPHE Lucien Goldmann, Barthes' standing as radical intellectual was questioned. In the moderate weekly magazine *L'Express*, Gérard Bonnot contrasted Barthes' response to May '68 to Goldmann's.[6] According to Bonnot, with his students qualified as 'elite' in their research activities, Barthes had been asking his students to collect marriage advertisements in the *Chasseur français* magazine (the French equivalent of *Hunting and Fishing*) for his linguistic research, but was now, in June 1968, in Bonnot's words, 'envisaging handing in his notice and leaving teaching'. Barthes' response to May '68 stood, wrote Bonnot, in direct opposition to Goldmann's excitement before the student movement. It was in the next number of *L'Express* that Barthes replied with a short letter in which he denied both of these suggestions, especially the idea that he had been 'using' his students to collate 'anything whatsoever' for his work – this would be important because much of Barthes' innovative seminar work in the early 1970s went on to rely on *le moissonnage*, the harvesting of students' experiences, ideas and thoughts (and an idea regularly used since in creative writing seminars everywhere).[7]

As well as his seminars at the EPHE being interrupted between May and October 1968, Barthes was largely overtaken by the events, preferring to support *Tel Quel*'s critique of the students' ultra-left actions as 'spontaneist'. Instead *Tel Quel*, especially Sollers and Marcelin Pleynet, put forward the idea – and Barthes repeated the suggestion in 'Writing the Event', his important essay in *Communications* in the number following May '68 – that what was needed to 'fissure' the 'social symbolic' was a much more long-term, theoretical fundamentalism, rather than the tokenistic revolt by students.[8] *Tel Quel* and Barthes' response to the 'failure' of May '68 – we must remember that within two months of the events taking place, the French Communist Party had encouraged everyone back to work with minor reforms won, allowing General de Gaulle, incredibly, to win the snap election in autumn 1968 – was to look towards the 'Orient' as a source of radical challenge. In *Tel Quel*'s case, the lead was given by Maoism, and by the China that emerged from the Cultural Revolution; for Barthes, it was Japan and its radically differing approach to the sign, to communication, to language. Indeed, the 1968 period saw Barthes' third visit to Japan, and it was here that the 'text Tokyo' (in Maurice Pinguet's words) began to take shape, though Barthes had taken no notes while there and had to reconstruct from memory.[9] In line with *Tel Quel*'s theoretical fundamentalism – what Patrick ffrench has called the 'Time of Theory' – Barthes had participated, in early 1968, in the GET seminars organized by *Tel Quel*, alongside Foucault and Jacques Derrida, but he maintained his theoretical independence in his seminar at the EPHE.[10]

Having begun a study of Balzac's highly curious, almost gothic short story 'Sarrasine' with his students in the postgraduate seminar at the EPHE in February 1968, Barthes realized, after the events of May '68, that his teaching, his seminar, his approach to research and to writing would never be the same again. Indeed, the first seminar back after the May '68 events, in November 1968, was introduced with a clear attempt by Barthes to situate the EPHE – and his seminar in particular – as a site of opposition to the technocratic solutions for research and university teaching being offered by the hastily drafted 'Edgar Faure Law' in the wake of the student uprising. As Barthes' seminar notes show, his reading of

Balzac's story now swiftly abandoned – or, at least, very heavily qualified – the structuralist approaches that he, and others, had been advocating during the first half of the 1960s.[11] Out went the 'model' as a way of approaching a text that he had proposed in his 'Introduction to the Structural Analysis of Narratives' in 1965. Gone also was any notion of a 'science' of a text; rather, Barthes made a radical shift in his critical practice: the science of literature was now, quite simply, writing.[12] The idea of a 'meta-language' – so useful in his semiological work on fashion in particular because it had allowed the researcher a space and a language outside of the object of study in which to account for it – was also superseded: all language deployed by the critic was now part of the problem of the language used in the (literary) text under consideration. This was a crucial development emerging from May '68, but, in Barthes' case, it was clearly under way before the events of that year. It is worth rewinding a short time, back to 1966, to appreciate the significance of Barthes' radical shift in the wake of May '68.

At the same time as writing *Criticism and Truth* in 1966, Barthes worked in his seminar at the EPHE on two (seemingly distinct) topics, the 'Discourse of History' and the 'Linguistics of Discourse'.[13] Not only did these two topics seem unconnected, but neither gave a hint of what Barthes was really suggesting and exploring in the seminar in 1966. One connection between the two was the topic of his previous seminar on the 'Old Rhetoric' in 1965, which displayed Barthes' strongly held view that since rhetoric – as a form of academic study – had been abandoned by the French education system in the 1870s, a new rhetoric was now needed.[14]

As we saw in our discussion of *Criticism and Truth*, Barthes was becoming aware in the mid-1960s of the radical plurality of meanings in a text. This stood in radical opposition to the monologic 'asymbolism' valorized by critical verisimilitude, to the 'clarity' and 'good taste' highlighted by traditional critics such as Raymond Picard and increasingly to the 'crisis of commentary' that even *la nouvelle critique* was overlooking. Building on the three pillars of his critical approach to a literary text developed since 1960 – parametrism, writing intransitively (or obliquely) and being a writer proper – Barthes theorized in the 1966–7 seminar what a piece of literary criticism would look like if it took on board these three requirements. The answer to this was not given in the 1966–7 seminar, but in the next seminar a year later. This seminar then became his 1970 essay *s/z*, which was the record of his reading in the seminar with his students of Balzac's 'Sarrasine', and moreover his *re*-writing of the story as an 'essay' a full 140 years after Balzac published his unsettling tale. Whereas the seminar of 1966 discussed, in purely hypothetical terms, the aim to '*re*-cover' the literary text in question with another (literary) 'text' – that of the critic – the seminar of 1968 on 'Sarrasine' put the idea into practice, with all the hesitations in the teaching situation that were then ironed out in the final essay *s/z*. As well as a prelude to the reading and rewriting of Balzac's tale in *s/z*, the seminar of 1966 led directly to one of Barthes' most famous and seminal articles, 'The Death of the Author', published first in English in the USA in autumn 1967 and not in French until November 1968, apparently delayed due to the events of May '68.[15]

The move from structuralism to post-structuralism was therefore well under way by 1966, but we must consider one further element in the 'Mutation' that Barthes saw taking place between pre- and post-'68. One other key meeting for Barthes in this period was following the 1967 arrival in Paris, from Bulgaria, of Julia Kristeva, who worked with Barthes and Goldmann.[16] Her introduction of the 'dialogic' and polyphonic theories of the Russian critic Mikhail Bakhtin completed the importation into France of the Russian 'formalist' tradition of the 1910s and '20s on which Barthes' colleague Tzvetan Todorov had been working during the 1960s. Bakhtin's theories also chimed with this critical moment in French intellectual history in which structuralism was suddenly seen as static and closed in its analysis, if not technocratic in its social politics. If we add the Bakhtinian insistence upon the body, discourse, subversion, hybridity, deviance, the popular 'carnivalesque', the decentred self and the materiality of the sign – all revealed to a French intelligentsia hungry for alternatives to structuralism – to the publication in 1966 of Jacques Lacan's seminar in psychoanalysis from the 1950s and early '60s, as well as to Derrida's two books of essays in 1967 (some of which were first published in *Tel Quel*), then structuralism's heyday was all but over.[17] Indeed, between October and November 1967, before his second visit to Japan, Barthes was a visiting professor at Johns Hopkins University in Baltimore, where, at a conference on contemporary theory and avant-garde popular culture, he spoke on the 'reality effect' in literature alongside Lacan, Todorov, Derrida and Georges Poulet.[18]

This conference is commonly seen as the moment when structuralism was replaced by post-structuralism – although this claim is somewhat ironic for a radical philosophy that famously ignores 'origins'. Indeed, though often considered high structuralist for its sustained use of semiology and taxonomy, Barthes' *The Fashion System*, also published in 1967, was arguably a post-structuralist text too, in that its use of semiology was beholden to the 'written' fashion item, and 'writing' (*écriture*) is a key term in this early post-structuralist phase; and the opening paragraphs of the essay on fashion dissolved the differences between author and scientist and suggested that semiology was already somewhat passé.[19]

It is important to stress then that May '68 and structuralism played out a complex relationship with each other. Non-structuralist colleagues associated with Barthes, such as Edgar Morin, Jean Duvignaud and André Glucksmann, were highly enthusiastic about the student revolt.[20] Both the students and structuralism aimed to question and reject the classical humanism of traditional institutions: the humanities, the Sorbonne, the synthesis of psychology and history. But apart from the work of Foucault – who was in Tunisia for the whole of May 1968 – most of structuralism was anathema to the students in revolt: Barthes, Lévi-Strauss and Greimas were all sidelined in favour of the sociologist Alain Touraine and the Marxist philosopher Henri Lefebvre, both leading the movement at Nanterre, and both anti-structuralist. The latter preferred the dialectic to the formalist pronouncements inspired by Saussure and semiology. But there were complexities even within Marxism. The sociologist René Lourau (a student of Lefebvre's) admired the work of Barthes, Jakobson, Lacan and Lévi-Strauss.[21] The phenomenologists, so often linked via Merleau-Ponty to semiology's perceived phenomenology, were also highly critical of structuralism, especially in the work of Paul Ricoeur and Emmanuel Lévinas. Above all, in philosophical and political terms, the intellectual who returned to dominate May '68, once eclipsed in the early 1960s by the structural Marxism of Communist Party renegade Louis Althusser, was Sartre. His ideas of group alienation and of 'serialization' chimed well with May '68, as Sartre championed the 'young' Marx, who had theorized alienation, over Althusser's 'later' Marx, who (so the argument went) had analysed how structures were stabilizing the system.[22] Indeed, Sartre was one of very few intellectuals there in May '68 who was listened to and not criticized. Barthes and the other structuralists mentioned above did not sign the letter published in the 10 May 1968 edition of *Le Monde* that denounced the brutal state repression of the students (whereas Sartre, Maurice Blanchot, André Gorz, Pierre Klossowski, Lacan, Lefebvre and Nadeau all did). Barthes announced that he was suspicious of the students' *gauchisme* (ultra-leftism), instead advocating a much more intellectual, rather than militant, critique of the system.[23]

One anecdote illustrated the gap between Barthesian theory and the student movement. At a student union meeting, while vaunting the utopian socialism of Charles Fourier, Barthes proposed, to guffaws from the radicalized students, a seminar on language and revolutionary action. Thus structuralism was seen as destroyed by May '68: history returned, we might say, to haunt this most anti-historical of approaches.

Both Barthes and *Tel Quel* had to accept critiques of their actions. Following a split in 1968, *Change* was set up as a rival journal by former Telquelian Jean-Pierre Faye as a counter to *Tel Quel*, which had been tightly linked to structuralism. Indeed, though Barthes agreed to join the *Tel Quel* visit to China in 1974, his own Marxism suggested a complex appreciation of *Tel Quel*. He was a fellow traveller rather than an editorial board member, involved with the journal more out of a friendship with Sollers and Kristeva than anything else (though we must not overlook his guarded enthusiasm for Maoist China in his 1971 essay in the *Times Literary Supplement*, 'Pax culturalis').[24] Indeed, the complexity of the times for the various strands of global Marxism were such that, in 'Réponses', the televised interview with Barthes in 1970 and 1971, Barthes made his position clear vis-à-vis May '68 and the Marxist tradition of his old friend Fournié (who died in 1968): 'Trotskyism from then had nothing to do with today's ultra-leftism (*gauchisme*) and its ideological excesses.'[25] This complexity would be extended by the deeply disappointing visit to Maoist China with Sollers, Pleynet, Kristeva and Wahl, as we shall see in the next chapter.

There must have been an immense effect on Barthes following May '68: to be a precursor, not just with *On Racine* and the Picard affair, but with *Mythologies* – so often seen as one of the key texts for the revolt (alongside writings by Herbert Marcuse, Raoul Vaneigem and Guy Debord, as well as Lefebvre) – only then to be roundly rejected. It was not, in fact, accurate to say that Barthes and his colleagues – rudely referred to by anti-Structuralists as 'Structures' – did not go onto the street in May '68. Indeed, Barthes' presence at the anti-Malraux demonstration in Paris in February 1968 in favour of Henri Langlois encouraged him to organize, with Violette Morin, a letter of support for Langlois on behalf of the EPHE on which his name was signed as a member of the 'Bureau' of the Comité de défense de la Cinémathèque – so much for Barthes' general lack of political commitment.[26] Indeed, Barthes would be a signatory to numerous open letters and petitions in the wake of May '68 and throughout the first half of the 1970s, especially in relation to gay rights and prisoners' rights.[27] And though his militancy had none of that of Foucault helping prisoners in the French penal system in the early 1970s, Barthes was never immune to socio-political questions. Nevertheless, Barthes felt disappointed (like many) by the outcome of May '68 generally, and in particular by the way in which he was characterized as part of the problem by the students in revolt. We should contrast this with Barthes' reception during a visit to the UK in January 1969, in which he was considered, possibly, as the new Sartre.

This comparison was an interesting one, since, in her biography, Marie Gil spends time matching Sartre and Barthes, especially in relation to their respective 'autobiographies' (*Les Mots* published in 1964 and *Roland Barthes by Roland Barthes* eleven years later) and to the question of narration versus fragment in biographical discourse. So the interview with Barthes in London for the *Sunday Times* in 1969, with the title 'Is Barthes the new Sartre?', must have raised a few eyebrows on the other side of the Channel.[28] Indeed, if Barthes was the new Sartre, it was only as a researcher and academic, Barthes being well known for his dislike and suspicion of the 'hysteria' typical of radical political militancy. In contrast, Sartre, photographed endlessly addressing workers and students in May '68, was soon to link up with the Maoists to form a new radical newspaper (*La Gauche prolétarienne*). Barthes displayed none of this enthusiasm, and it may be that the pessimistic conclusions of 'Myth Today' at the end of *Mythologies* had predicted not so much May '68 but its failure, the unexpected political fallout. What was often referred to as the 'recuperation' of May '68 had been presciently theorized ten years before by Barthes in the ability of myth to latch onto anything: May '68 could be – and has been, to some extent – 'recuperated' by the very system it had set out to challenge, hence the need felt by Barthes in 1970 to write a new preface for the second edition of *Mythologies*.[29] May '68's 'failure' – quotation marks required, as the social effects of the events of May '68 are very easy to underestimate – encouraged Barthes to see opposition as mainly ideological, literary and aesthetic. It is not surprising that one of the most inspiring aspects of May '68 for Barthes was the extraordinary explosion of graffiti – often witty, inspired and even poetic – on walls all over central Paris. The wall being 'the fundamental place of collective writing', Barthes keenly contrasted radical writing with the (populism of) students wanting to 'have a voice'.[30]

His seminar at the EPHE would henceforth be the site of, the space for, this social and political critique. From 1968 to 1975,

'Culture is the opposite of LIFE'. His injunction to 'Write everywhere!' illustrated Barthes' enthusiasm for May '68 graffiti.

opposition would be led, ideologically and aesthetically, by Barthes in intellectual discussion with his postgraduate students. The fact that the seminar was interrupted in May '68 did not stop Barthes, on his return in November that year, from underlining the century-long oppositional role that the EPHE had played from its inception in 1868 onwards; the almost sacred space that was Barthes' seminar at the EPHE in the early 1970s was underlined by his 1974 paean to the class and to his students.[31]

It was not simply the *gauchiste* students – who were, needless to say, not the postgraduate students in his seminar – who drew Barthes' staunch critique. Hippies were also given the semiologist's treatment, in an article published in *Communications* in 1969 that Barthes wrote in Morocco. Barthes' time in Morocco was spent as a *coopérant* at Mohammed V University, in the capital of newly independent Morocco. Much of what we know of Barthes' time in Morocco comes from the set of notes and laconic impressions, *Incidents*, published posthumously in 1987. As a sort of writer's notebook, *Incidents* is sometimes relatively shocking in the off-hand

A seminar led by Barthes at L'École pratique des hautes études (EPHE), Paris, 1975.

and vulgar way in which Barthes detailed daily life. As a personal record, in part, of meetings with young Moroccan boys for amorous relations, one can only speculate over whether Barthes would have allowed its publication. Indeed, *Incidents* is followed by *Soirées de Paris* (Paris Evenings), a rather depressing set of writer's notes written in (and about) Paris soon after the death of his beloved mother in 1977. François Wahl, Barthes' literary executor at the Seuil publishing house, was roundly criticized for allowing these (surprisingly) frank notes to be given public space. Not only very personal – showing a European literary self at large in a sexually charged, postcolonial situation – *Incidents* is certainly not the best place to start reading Barthes' work. This is not to say that the notes have no merit: critics have noted the 'photographic' way in which Barthes' note form in *Incidents* records, in fragments and almost aphoristically, the different social situations and daily interactions using the light touch of a writer.

Invited to work in Rabat by the Moroccan poet Zaghloul Morsy, Barthes established important friendships in Morocco. He wrote a rare essay on poetry that theorized the linguistic 'table-turning' undertaken by Morsy's extraordinary 1969 poem 'D'un soleil réticent'; Barthes' conclusion that French people could now see that the French language was actually 'foreign' to the French, since Morsy's use of it sent a new French back to France, was an idea that prefigured much of Barthes' appreciation of another Moroccan poet and theorist, Abdelkebir Khatibi.[32] Nevertheless, Barthes' experience of Morocco was, on balance, not a positive one, and he ended his three-year contract after only one year. There was at least a good reason for this. Barthes was not paid in Rabat, as he was the equivalent of a lowly university lecturer without the required further academic qualifications. Furthermore, not only was he missing his mother, but he arrived just as the period of Morocco's notorious *Années de plomb* in 1969–73 was starting, with students in revolt against Hassan II and the postcolonial French influence in

Morocco. So the radical Barthes (the new Sartre?) whom we saw in London in January 1969, arrived in Morocco in September of the same year, to teach Proust, Verne and Poe – hardly revolutionary stuff! Despite his friends at *Tel Quel* – Sollers, Kristeva and Pleynet – moving towards Maoist politics and 'burning' bourgeois literature as they went, as Barthes put it, he nevertheless rejected the Maoism of his Moroccan students and ignored their disappointment that a *Tel Quel* fellow traveller would elect to teach them Proust![33] The Moroccan students preferred Lucien Goldmann to Barthes' literary (read: 'bourgeois') approach, and Moroccan students boycotted his teaching of Claudel's *Le Soulier de satin* (The Satin Slipper), deeming it a colonialist play.[34] However, as often with his sojourns abroad (in Bucharest and then in Alexandria), Barthes made good use of the time that he had in Morocco. It was the boredom and ennui of his experience that allowed him to have lengthy discussions with a new friend he had made in Rabat, Michel Bouvard, who was developing his interest in photography and whose doctoral work on photography Barthes would supervise once back in Paris.

If Morocco showed a somewhat compromised, and bored, Barthes, Japan was the perfect counterpoint to all that we know in the 'West'. In an uncanny copy of Brecht's epic theatre, Japan was discovered by Barthes to be a society where it would seem that, unlike in the West, meaning was clear, fixed and ritualized. *Empire of Signs*, published in 1970 by Geneva-based Skira in its innovative and glossy series *Les Sentiers de la création* (The Paths of Creation), was, interestingly, Barthes' first *true* book, in the sense that his other books so far – *Writing Degree Zero*, *Michelet*, *Mythologies*, *On Racine*, *Critical Essays* – were all collections of previously published (usually journalistic) pieces; *Criticism and Truth*, *The Fashion System* and *s/z* were 'academic' essays.

As a 'record' of his visits to Japan in the second half of the 1960s, *Empire of Signs* is a curious text. Indeed, when we consider the efforts that his maternal grandfather, Louis Binger, made in his writings on West Africa to 'know' local Mossi and Kong tribal cultures, his grandson's stark refusal to enter into Japanese culture is quite striking. Perhaps, however, this was one of Barthes' points, brilliantly elaborated by the French-Caribbean writer Édouard Glissant in his work on ethnography in the 1990s: namely, that in understanding a culture – Glissant plays on the word for understanding in French, *comprendre*, which has *prendre* (to take) within it – one risked 'taking' it.[35] The 'distance' that Barthes established between himself (but also the West, Europe and so on) on the one hand, and Japan on the other, made *Empire of Signs* into an oppositional text, in that it took a distant country and showed how its system of cultural and social signs (meals, gift-giving, dress and daily customs) were thoroughly 'open', healthy and self-consciously artificial, especially when compared to the 'unhealthy', artificial sign in the West. Japan had a signifying system in all aspects of life that, to the eyes of a Westerner such as Barthes – who was used to the hypocrisy of the sign, especially in its participation in connotation and mystification – could only be apprehended by remaining on the 'surface' of Japanese cultural and communicational systems. By not knowing the Japanese language, by standing apart from its 'babble' of communication, Barthes, the essayist, could mobilize this somewhat 'fictitious' culture on the other side of the world that he described from a distance – from the outside, as it were – as a critique of Western society.

Thus in *Empire of Signs* he brought together all the theoretical and critical ideas that he had deployed in his career so far: Brechtian 'distance', Micheletian sensitivity to popular culture, semiological and anthropological analysis of social functions, and Marxian understanding of ideology and critique of Western orthodoxies. But there was certainly one area – which we will explore in more detail in the final two chapters – that we might wish to consider as a major development in Barthes' work: his getting beyond the literalist/metaphorical opposition between the terms of which

Barthes was happy to oscillate in the 1950s and early '60s. Now, under the influence of Zen philosophy, he began to theorize areas beyond the binary oppositions so favoured by structuralism and semiology. Emptiness, the void (*mu* in Japanese) led Barthes to explore the most recondite aspect of communication: namely, silence – that is, the exemption of, and suspension of, meaning. Naturally, if one did not know the Japanese language, one had the advantage of not getting caught up in the 'signifieds' – or meanings – of speech and communication, thereby allowing a freedom to explore the rich range of signifiers, which, to a Japanese person, generated those very meanings; and these meanings were bracketed thanks to Barthes' linguistic incapacity in Japanese.

Barthes' 'Brechtian' reading of Japanese culture had begun in his essay on Japanese theatre in *Tel Quel*, 'Lesson in Writing', which appeared in the number immediately after the May '68 events and was to become the basis of 'The Three Writings' in *Empire of Signs*.[36] In drama terms, Japanese *bunraku* theatre was like the 'modern text' – that is, 'citational' – constantly saying things between speech marks and openly self-conscious of its own artistic medium, precisely what the Barthes of *s/z* was wanting to find in the 'writable' text, subsumed as it was under the 'readability' requirements of the literary market. Barthes' writing on Japan suggested a new positivity in his work; *Empire of Signs* also initiated what seemed to be a new literary genre, a *fiction théorique* (theoretical fiction) that would go on to dominate Barthes' books for the rest of his career.

Empire of Signs was well received in France, but Barthes' other book of 1970, *s/z*, left many critics unimpressed. Lévi-Strauss, true to form in his disparaging views on Barthes, considered Barthes' reading of Balzac's story, rather uncharitably given the recent 'Picard affair', to be similar to the 'Racine' by Müller and Reboux.[37] But Barthes' reading of Balzac's story in *s/z* must be seen as part of a second wave in the reception of Ferdinand de Saussure's theories on semiology and language. In the 1950s researchers interested in semiology, such as Greimas, Merleau-Ponty and then Barthes, had worked hard to introduce Saussure's theories not just to literary critics but to linguistics specialists more generally. While battles were raging over the value of semiology – of Saussure's view that meaning operates 'differentially' – the 1960s saw the introduction of a different, more mystical and less formalist Saussure. Thanks to the work of Jean Starobinski, researchers in the mid-1960s began to explore Saussure's theory of anagrams.[38] In short, Saussure had worked tirelessly towards the end of his life trying to prove that texts, possibly all texts, had hidden, encoded messages – *paragrammes* – that were woven into, or under, their surface meanings; from the close study of religious texts, such as the Old Testament, to more modern writings, Saussure had nearly gone mad by believing that he could 'hear' coded messages, his job being to reveal their deeper meanings.

The influence of these anagrammatic approaches could be felt in post-structuralism, and in the work of Julia Kristeva (on avant-garde poetry and theories of the novel) in particular, but also in the wider cult of the letter (the written figure and the form of correspondence) that post-structuralism inaugurated, especially through Derrida's insistence on the pre-eminence of writing in relation to speech. There was indeed a good example in Barthes' work – according to Gil, it comes in the title of the essay *s/z*. Not so much psychobiography on her part as 'fictional' biography, Gil's account of Barthes' psychoanalytical 'hole' tries to show not how we 'read' Barthes' life from his texts but rather how Barthes inscribes in his texts cryptic, even fictionalized, references to himself. So the illicit affair that Barthes' mother had had with married man André Salzedo (whose wife, an artist, changed her name to Salcedo after her divorce) led to the birth of Barthes' half-brother Michel Salzedo. Did Barthes therefore weave, as Gil and Éric Marty strongly suggest, this psychoanalytical event into *s/z*, just as Saussure had 'heard' other messages in his anagrams? Or is it simply that Marty and Gil are also 'hearing' this?[39]

Indeed, much of the interpretation of Barthes' *s/z* has revolved around the psychoanalytical dimensions to the Balzac story – following Jean Reboul's seminal, psychoanalytical reading of Balzac's 'Sarrasine' – highlighting the manner in which Barthes set up paradigmatic bars between characters in the story, locating the story's drive in the post-Freudian, explicitly Lacanian, notion of lack. This analysis of human drives and voids then relies heavily on the narrative analysis of Balzac's tale that Barthes' essay performed – above all, by equating the different levels of narration (contractual and sexual, on one level, undecidable and open on another) and by de-hierarchizing the various competing 'entry points' to the story.[40] This concentration on the psychoanalytical and narratological dimensions of Barthes' reading – and rewriting – of Balzac's 'Sarrasine' comes, it would seem, at the expense of the other, Marxian category that Barthes' essay and the recently published seminar notes of 1968–9 traced in Balzac's story. This 'economic' theme revolved around what Barthes called the 'inorigin' of money. It was not so much an 'ex-nomination' that Barthes now underscored, as he had done in relation to the bourgeoisie in the *Mythologies* essay 'Myth Today'; rather, it was a naming of the subtle financial and social connotations that key words in Balzac's story generated. Early in the story and early in Barthes' commentary (lexis number 4), the clock sounding midnight on the Elysée Bourbon was deemed to be a 'metonymy' that leads to the meaning 'Wealth':

> This wealth is itself connoted: a neighbourhood of *nouveaux riches*, the Faubourg Saint-Honoré refers by synecdoche to the Paris of the Bourbon Restoration, a mythic place of sudden fortunes whose origins are suspect; where gold is produced without an origin, diabolically (the symbolic definition of speculation).[41]

It is almost as if Barthes saw a socio-historical parallel between 1830 on the one hand – when the nobility's conspicuous and often obscene wealth had been, following the French Revolution and the failed restoration of the monarchy in 1830, newly re-codified by the ascendant (and now-triumphant) bourgeoisie into 'new money' – and, on the other, modern France of 1960, where social class (in short, where one got one's money from in order to live) had become hidden beneath a complex layer of social practices, uneven meritocracy and blurred social identities.[42] We must not forget that not only had Barthes studied (if only briefly), in the early 1950s, the political and social language of 1825–35, he had written a wonderful essay in 1962 on the nineteenth-century dandy, which linked the social changes in class across the nineteenth century (the final triumph of the bourgeoisie and the curbing of aristocratic power) to the new style of dress, the (social) distinction afforded by vestimentary detail, that the dandy inaugurated.[43] In *s/z* Barthes then followed the untraceable but connoted origins of the Lanty family's wealth through Balzac's story until he equated 'inorigin of wealth' – empty, as it was – with castration, 'the physiological impossibility of procreating'. And this 'inorigin' was also linked to the narrative voice in Balzac's story, which (rather like the Cheshire Cat's smile in *Alice's Adventures in Wonderland*) seemed to come 'from' no one or nowhere. As Barthes pointed out, the 'inorigin' of voices in the Balzac story had a particular effect on the interpretation of the text: 'The more indeterminate the origin of the statement, the more plural the text.'[44]

In terms of Barthes' own life then, as well as the possible codification of his family tensions in relation to his half-brother Michel, *s/z* was also a (historical?) materialist attempt to point not so much to the class setting of Balzac's story, but rather to the (utopian) belief in the possibility of not being socially determined, or 'classified' in social terms. Needless to say, this theme of escaping classification is one that has guided our account of Barthes' life so

Barthes in Nice, 1972.

far, and one way to escape classification that Barthes would increasingly underline for us all was to enter into the world of writing. *s/z* gestured then towards the social reading of Balzac's story that had taken place in the EPHE seminar between February 1968 and January 1969 (the essay's epigraph dedicated the book to the attentive students in the seminar); in addition, the main aim of *s/z* was to show that reading must generate the desire to write. Crucially, one of the major social drives emerging in Barthes' experience of the 1960s was the radical idea that in order to read you need to write. In other words, the radical reading of text, of society, of the self, must pass through writing: from the popular theatre movement to the disalienation of society's objects in *Mythologies*, and from the 'degree zero' thesis's insistence on the socially inflected nature of literary form to Michelet's lost masses in history, Barthes' aim to get everyone to 'write' (considered by some to be a utopian ideal, and others a provocative call) – in order to 'read' – fitted with his sensitivity to the excluded, to the 'masses' and to a (or some) sense of social justice. If May '68 had brought this radical, writerly idea to the fore, then the period following May '68 – what Barthes called the 'Mutation' – would see him now go on to explore and advocate it further.

6

From the *École* to the *Collège*

Back in France in 1970, after the shortened stay in Morocco, Barthes found a new, more modern France: new journals and universities had emerged, and the humanities had been replaced by *sciences humaines*. From Morocco and from Japan, Barthes brought back a fascination with calligraphy, with the letter and with the signifier, all elements typical of the 'cult' of writing that characterized post-structuralism. It is no coincidence that Barthes' first watercolour paintings date from June 1971, and, by the end of his life, his paintings amounted to 700 in total. Painting and calligraphy are, in their lightness of touch, like playing the piano, which was Barthes' passion throughout his life. Indeed, whether it be in painting or music, the 'amateur' (literally, the 'person who loves') – an important status for the late Barthes, in that it undermines both professionalism and the institutionalized control of leisure – could produce a *graphie pour rien* (pointless tracing), what he called a *pulsion graphique*, between which Barthes would soon supersede binary modes of thought and find the neutral. The 'amateur', Barthes suggested, would be the only status of those who write once a truly 'disalienated' society is reached.[1]

Many of his drawings were made for Romaric Sülger-Buel, a friend of painter-dealer Daniel Cordier at whose house in Juan-les-Pins (on the other side of southern France from Barthes' adopted Bayonne) Barthes wrote his *Roland Barthes by Roland Barthes*, the cover of which, *Souvenirs de Juan-les-Pins*, is one of his crayon

Barthes began painting as a hobby in 1971, inspired by Japanese calligraphy.

drawings from 1974. Not only were painting and drawing a way
for Barthes to achieve a certain Buddhist mandala – a ritualized
set of graphic actions that precede more meaningful work – they
were an opportunity to concentrate on the signifier, at the expense
of the signified. Normally in linguistics, the letter does not signify
(the moneme or the morpheme are the smallest units of meaning);
but for Barthes, and for psychoanalysis in which everything
signified, the letter became central from 1971 onwards. For
example, Barthes wrote a startling commentary in 1971 on the
avant-garde alphabet drawn by fashion designer Erté.[2] Indeed,
the 'plural' of the text that had dominated his work on 'Sarrasine'
in 1970 had now become an interest in the duplicity of language,
emerging both from Saussure's work on hidden anagrams and
from the significant number of *add'ad* – also known as *enantiosemes*
(to give them their full linguistic name) or contronyms, single

words that contain two directly opposing meanings – that Barthes encountered in Arabic while in Morocco.[3]

There was also a double-sidedness to Barthes' experience of wider exposure in the media in the early 1970s. His burgeoning fame in 1971 was such that that year saw the first-ever book about his writing and the first journal issue devoted to him.[4] But Barthes still had to contend with the popularity of his seminar at the EPHE, having, finally, to increase the policing of those students who were not signed up, and changing the venue. It was in this period that the cinema theorist Christian Metz and the literary theorist Gérard Genette were regular participants in his popular seminar. It led Seuil, in 1972, to publish a second collection of his essays, *New Critical Essays*, which also contained a new, second edition of *Writing Degree Zero*. The same year, he was invited by Jacques Le Goff (who had recently replaced Fernand Braudel as head of the EPHE) to be part of the management of the EPHE, which included seeing through the change of name in 1974 to the École des hautes études en sciences sociales (EHESS).

Despite his struggles with growing fame and notoriety at this time, Barthes also began to feel more comfortable in his social milieu. He made friends with the film-maker André Techiné; with a young philosophy student of Lefebvre's, Jean-Louis Bouttes; and with a future culture minister under President Mitterrand, Jack Lang, who, in 1974, was the director of the Chaillot theatre in Paris (and who would invite Barthes in 1980 to the fateful lunch with Mitterrand after which Barthes was accidently knocked down and subsequently died). Nevertheless, Barthes' increasing fame brought the possibility of embarrassment, especially in relation to his (largely hidden) homosexuality. In 1971 Georges Lapassade, whom Barthes had met in Morocco, published a novel, *Le Bordel andalou* (The Andalusian Brothel), in which the homosexual character Roland Putois was shown to be a hypocrite by his very different behaviour in the hammam on the one hand and in the public square on the other; and Barthes had to act swiftly when, in the same year, another writer alluded to his homosexuality.[5]

As his fame grew, so did the urge to consider the self and the subject within the rubble of structuralist and post-structuralist theories, which, since the 1950s and especially in the wake of May '68, had largely undermined liberal and humanist accounts of human identity. Aware of the dangers of valorizing writing over speech, and keen to underscore the realities of the body, of the voice and of performance, Barthes developed his passion for singing and music in his essay writing.[6] *Sade, Fourier, Loyola* in 1971 was the first major work of this new 'biographical' period. As well as exploring a deconstructed, and decentred, notion of self, Barthes began to apply his theories on text to the self.[7] If the self was constituted in human society differentially, as both Lacan and Saussure in their own ways implied, then it was via the linguistic 'text' – language – that this self was to be best apprehended, hence Barthes' interest in three very different writers, all of whom were 'logothets', inventors of new ways of writing: the pornographer Marquis de Sade, the utopian socialist Charles Fourier and the Jesuit mystic Ignatius Loyola. However, typical of Barthes, things were not quite as simple as this. As well as inventing new ways to apprehend the world in language, two of the three writers (Sade and Fourier) revealed (inadvertently, it would seem) distinct biographical signifiers about themselves – 'biographemes'. For Barthes, these small, largely insignificant pieces of information were based on the key discovery of his work on fashion, the 'detail'.

In his writings on fashion, Barthes showed that a whole fashion outfit could be (almost infinitely) re-combined and re-directed, especially if a small (change of) detail was included.[8] This was a typically post-structuralist account of social phenomena (in that it was a micro-structure that was seen to affect the macro-structure), whereby the 'combinatory' possibilities between different structures were catalysed by the tiniest of phenomena. In terms of the writings of Sade, Fourier and Loyola – and not forgetting the 'combination' that these very disparate writers created when they were brought together – the 'detail' was the over-concentration on aspects of life (the smell of dirty linen or the interminable lists of the exact debauched pleasures for Sade, the precise manners with which the utopian socialists lived their days communally in the phalanstery for Fourier or the 'dialectical' ways in which praying engaged with both time and the sign of God for Loyola). The 'detail' then, as Barthes imagined it in *Sade, Fourier, Loyola*, was the route through which the self could constitute, and finally know, itself. Such was the radical scepticism in early 1970s France towards individual and unified – that is, unproblematic – accounts of the self that there was no going back to the 'full', humanist subject; hence Barthes' solution (albeit provisional) to re-finding the self (with all the Micheletian connotations of 'resurrection' as a corrective to social exclusion) was to make life as a text.[9] So Sade, Fourier and Loyola were not biographied as such, but their lives, via their writings and Barthes' own fictions and fantasies, were given over to what Barthes called the 'romanesque', the novelistic.[10] The 'romanesque' was the fictional, in essay form, before it became a novel or a fiction proper, so that each of his three chosen authors returned as a plural set of charms. As Barthes would suggest in his final set of lectures in 1979–80, the 'romanesque' was a 'life as work', and Barthes even admitted that the biography of a writer was more interesting than his work sometimes.[11]

This mixture of the 'romanesque' and the biographical detail gleaned from a writer's text, the 'biographeme', led to a 'pleasure of the text', which was precisely the title of Barthes' next essay, published in 1973. The title contained much of the psychoanalysis that Barthes had been employing in his work, but the essay itself indicated clearly how, from at least 1972 onwards, it was the work of Friedrich Nietzsche that was guiding his writing style. Barthes' trademark style was now the fragment, elliptical, suggestive and

unconventional in its form; the *moralité* that he advocated in
The Pleasure of the Text was no longer beholden to Montaigne but
to the fragmented and aphoristic style of the German philosopher.
Alongside Nietzsche and Marx, Barthes also applied the theories
of Freud.[12] Thus *The Pleasure of the Text* was a critique of the *lieu
commun* (commonplace) in pleasure, whereby neither the left wing
nor the right showed pleasure to be 'atopic'. Making the important
(psychoanalytical) distinction between pleasure (*plaisir*) and ecstasy
(*jouissance*), Barthes mobilized theories on perversion derived from
Freud and which he had developed in his 1972 seminar at the EPHE
on Freud.

Though this late phase of Barthes' career was well prepared by
all that came before, there was a subtle shift in Barthes' interests
and obsessions. Language – no longer (or, not so much) a medium
of ideological theft (or 'myth'), nor (so much) the site of the critic's
direct engagement with text via rewriting that we have considered
so far – was now appreciated, studied, deconstructed, for the
very conditions in which it placed humans. In typical post-'68
fashion, Barthes linked language and love. In the 'Réponses'
interview from 1970–71, he began to look back over his career
for the first time and described the various phases as a series of
disinvestments in all things, except language, for which the choice
of analogy was as amusing as it was telling: language was, opined
Barthes, a bit like being in love with someone all these years but
trying out new erotic positions. Obviously, we should not take
this too literally, but it underscored well his attitude to his own
hypersensitivity to language: 'I have a disease: I *see* language',
he famously declared in *Roland Barthes by Roland Barthes*.[13] In
the same year, 1975, he went even further with his view of the
fundamental, even foundational, nature of language, by which he
now meant not so much communication in general – semiology,
signs and non-verbal social intercourse – but the 'performance'
of self via the verbal.

In his 1975 essay 'The Rustle of Language' (also the title given to a posthumous set of essays published in 1984), he set out the 'health' of language as a *bruissement* – the sound of an engine running smoothly (and perhaps not best translated into English as 'rustle'). He ended on a deeply stark, human note:

> I imagine myself today something like the ancient Greek as Hegel describes him: he interrogated, Hegel says, passionately, uninterruptedly, the rustle of branches, of springs, of winds, in short the shudder of Nature, in order to perceive in it the design of an intelligence. And I – it is the shudder of meaning that I interrogate, listening to the rustle of language, that language which for me, modern man, is my Nature.[14]

At the same time as this shift towards a foundational view of language, Barthes, as we have noted, began one of the final stages of his consideration of image, of the self. However, as always for an oscillator – and the attitude to language above was very much an example of this oscillation – Barthes both played on, and, at the same time, conjured away his own image. This is important for two reasons: first, Barthes began to feel self-conscious about his 'self', especially following the heightened media attention of the 1968 period onwards. Régis Debray's 'age of the intellectual' described a mediatized intellectual post-1968, and this description was very much true of Barthes, who had become a regular interviewee not just in the press and the radio throughout the 1970s, but crucially he had been interviewed in 1977 on television, on the popular literary show *Apostrophes*. But if Barthes acceded to a kind of intellectual 'guru' status in the 1970s, albeit a minor one compared to Foucault, Derrida, Deleuze and Sartre, he was keen, throughout this final decade of his life, to dissolve, if not lose, the self. Second, and crucial for his writing projects, his 'playing-out' of the self – in seminars, in *Roland Barthes by Roland Barthes* and in *A Lover's Discourse* – had to, if it was to avoid the charge of arrogance, egotism or decadence, 'decentre' itself across language and writing.

The most startling example of this impersonalism was the use of the third person in his biography of himself in *Roland Barthes by Roland Barthes*, typified by the injunction at the start of it that 'all this' should be considered as 'spoken by a character in a novel'. In other words, all that was said about 'Roland Barthes' in *Roland Barthes by Roland Barthes* needed to be taken, not so much with a pinch of salt (it was not a set of lies, embellishments nor even a faithful 'picture'), but as an experiment in standing 'outside' of oneself (as if it were a novel in the third person), while knowing, intimately, the person concerned. The seminar at the EPHE in 1973–4 (published in 2009) was the origin of this tactical bracketing, or exteriorizing, of self.[15]

Barthes even went so far as to apply this exteriorizing of self in the article that he wrote for *Le Monde* (an important moderate daily in France) following his return from the *Tel Quel*-led tour of China in April and May 1974. Visiting Beijing, Sian, Shanghai, Nanking and Luo Yang under tight security – in a Maoist China that had not quite finished the 'Cultural Revolution' begun in 1966 – Barthes and his *Tel Quel* friends were ostensibly on a politico-cultural fact-finding mission. This period was one in which the French Communist Party was losing its grip on the labour movement and the Left generally; it had betrayed the movement in 1968, and the Gulag camps that had supposedly ended with Stalin's era were returned to the front page by Solzhenitsyn in 1970. So China, for a short period, from 1966 to 1974, became an alternative guide in world revolutionary politics, alongside its ideological offshoot, Guevarism. From Morocco to Indonesia, the success of Mao's Red Book – underpinned by China's involvement in the 1960s Vietnam War against the USA – was such that students in revolt waved the book at demonstrations, and France was no different. A small but significant Maoist grouping developed in the early

1970s in France, in a movement backed by Jean-Paul Sartre, the remnants of which survive, today, in the newspaper *Libération*; *Tel Quel*, with its fascination with Chinese and East Asian culture, was well placed to play a part in the opening of relations in the West following U.S. President Nixon's visit to China in 1971.

Barthes' diary of his visit, with Philippe Sollers and Julia Kristeva (now secretly married), the poet Marcelin Pleynet and the Seuil editor François Wahl, has recently been published in France.[16] It is a fascinating account of what turned out to be a failure. Not only was China *not* Japan for Barthes – *fade* (dull and boring), coded in a controlling way – it was a thoroughly unfree society, in essence no different from the Stalinized Romania of Barthes' youth. Much of the *carnets* (notebooks) recorded Barthes' constant boredom and frustration at getting straight, useful facts about the progressive nature, or otherwise, of Mao's Cultural Revolution; the frustration was greater for his *Tel Quel* colleagues, evident especially in the brief but observant descriptions by Barthes of Sollers in full Maoist mode.[17] However, it was the article and in particular the title 'Alors, la Chine?' ('So, What about China?), published in *Le Monde* in late May 1974, that underlined the social way in which Barthes performed and recorded his experiences and analyses. Indeed, Barthes 'gave' his visit to China as a seminar in 1974, attaching it to the idea of the 'writer's lexis'.[18] Without it being arrogant, Barthes' title for his 'response' to China on his return to Paris gestured towards his indisputable intellectual fame in mid-1970s France. 'So, What about China?' displayed all the stylistic hallmarks of his undergoing a media interrogation in its spoken informality and its rhetorical device. And what was Barthes' (rhetorical) reply? Nothing. 'We' (that is, Barthes and *Tel Quel*) have come back from China with 'nothing'.[19] Not since André Gide visited the Soviet Union in the 1930s had the responses of intellectuals been so sought after as those following this trip to China in 1974 – and Barthes offered 'nothing', or very little. In a typical 'suspension of judgement',[20] Barthes regretted the way in which Chinese society showed texts that were 'only' political: posters, ideological phrases and turns of speech (*briques*) were used interminably, as part of a Marxist 'vulgate' that would please any *apparatchik* of the Stalin era in the Soviet Union or of the French Communist Party in the 1970s under Georges Marchais. The whole trip was a failure then, as China never emerged beyond the simplistic repetition of Red Book slogans. Indeed, this 'vulgate' of Marxism experienced in China would encourage Barthes, in 1977, to question the long-term viability of Marxism once it had been adopted en masse.

It is also important to underline the influence of this 'suspension' on Barthes' use of Taoism. Increasingly, Barthes saw his role not as a prominent intellectual – whose opinion should be solicited and, crucially, given on every matter in society – but as a critical voice 'in retreat'. This was not so much retreat in the political sense in the 1970s – though there was a a deep sense of malaise in the period that accompanied the slow re-stabilization of French capitalism after May '68 – but retreat in the sense of Brecht's injunction to 'liquidate and theorize', of tactical acts of defiance, such as refusing to comment openly on Mao's China in *Le Monde*. This was theorized in his lecture series called (appropriately enough) *The Neutral*, following the Taoist idea of *wou-wei*, which, as 'inaction' or 'refusal to choose', was deemed by Barthes to be a 'powerful subversion of all of our moral values, and notably of the "progressive ones"'.[21] This was the measure in the mid-1970s not only of Barthes' 'detached' critique of society but of the extent to which radical left-wing ideas seemed, at the time, to have run out of steam. It was no doubt also a measure of the power of the education system to 'recuperate' – that is, to co-opt and thereby nullify the energy attached to radicalism – that which seemed to be undermining it. Thus Barthes, like Foucault in his 'inaugural lecture' to the Collège de France published as *L'Ordre du discours* (Paris, 1971), considered subversion now to be possible only from the 'inside', in Barthes' version no longer by the 'critique' typical of *Mythologies* (which was by now, in mid-1970s France, which was part of the technocratic university's skill set) but by 'theft', by the 'play' within the system, part of a surreptitious chipping away at the symbolic order on which Western civilization relied.

Despite the 'recuperation' operated by the education system of those radically challenging the system, one of the 'gains' of the 1960s was that the academy felt obliged to open up beyond the narrow limits provided by the traditionalism of a Sorbonne professor such as Raymond Picard. Foucault and Barthes, having played their role in the reorganization of the higher education system in France, were set to benefit from the integration – some might say 'recuperation' – of the radical structuralist and post-structuralist theories emerging from the 1960s. Foucault, in his post at the prestigious Collège de France since 1970, invited Barthes to join him there. Barthes was to replace the recently deceased Hellenist Louis Robert (the custom at the Collège de France being that the person who is replaced must be name-checked by the replacement in his inaugural lecture). Neither Georges Dumézil nor the Collège seemed to want the *mondain* (socialite) Barthes, and, though successful, the vote for Barthes' election to the Collège de France was apparently a very close call. But Barthes had made it to a chair in Literary Semiology at the Collège de France, where Paul Valéry had lectured thirty years before. The appointment gave Barthes the opportunity to develop further his research on, and attitude towards, language.

In his inaugural lecture at the Collège, published as 'Leçon', Barthes made two key claims: first, as a 'patently impure fellow', he was also 'of doubtful nature, whose every attribute is somehow challenged by its opposite'; second – and oft quoted out of context – he suggested that 'Language . . . is quite simply fascist.' The qualifier that follows is 'for fascism does not prevent speech, it compels speech'.[22] As someone regularly solicited for his opinion in the media, Barthes was looking in 1977 for a way to remain silent – to suspend judgement – and therefore, despite his deep fascination with language, Barthes pointed also to its oppressive nature. This dialectical – or oscillatory – view of language was exemplified in the essay on a lover's discourse that was published the same year as his nomination for a chair at the Collège.

A Lover's Discourse and its prologue underlined perfectly the dialectic of the social/solitary in Barthes' work to the extent that amorous discourse – in as much as it is 'warranted by none' (ignored, mocked and not part of 'gregarity') – was deemed to be 'affirmative'. So the 'extreme solitude' of lovers' discourse was, in good oscillatory (or non-resolved dialectical) fashion, a deep form of social intercourse (albeit normally reserved for two people in a relationship). Just as it was impossible, following Barthes' analysis of Edgar Allan Poe's story 'The Facts in the Case of M. Valdemar', to say 'I am dead', it was meaningless (a zero-degree meaning?) to say 'I love you' without affirming the existence of the Other.[23] One might object that this is not so much 'social' as 'non-individual', but this is a discussion we might leave to philosophers: the key point was that the self, as Barthes showed it, was never alone, even in its extreme solitude, for, though the self all alone sat outside of the normative notion of the 'performance' of self in relation to the presence of the Other, it was still deeply connected to the social via the unconscious. This situation became all the more paradoxical when Barthes started his final seminar topic at the EPHE (now renamed the EHESS), a two-year investigation between 1974 and 1976 into the language and speech of love.[24]

That *A Lover's Discourse*, the book with the highest sales in Barthes' oeuvre, has been turned into a play speaks volumes on the deeply social nature of Barthes' project.[25] Rather than seeing love as a singularly personal experience, *A Lover's Discourse* showed how lovers play out a set of social constraints and limited freedoms via a language that is unknown (and unknowable, even) to scientific and humanistic knowledge. If one were to try to trace the 'personal' realities that Barthes invested in *A Lover's Discourse* – names of lovers tantalizingly left as initials, for example – it would be to miss the point.[26] Language, as the central theme in *A Lover's Discourse*, *de*specified the deeply personal experience of amorous interaction with the Other, as if 'language' itself were in love, rather than the speaking human being the subject of love. Not surprisingly, Barthes used a range of texts – mainly literary, such as Goethe's *Werther*, Proust and Flaubert, but also Freud, Lacan, Nietzsche and D. W. Winnicott – all put together, in an alphabetical order of 'figures' that merely hid the wandering, erratic nature of the essayistic fragments that had come to define Barthes' writing. Not so much arbitrary as falsely scientific, the alphabetical order was a key technique in breaking any 'continuous', or organized, approach that might imply a hierarchy. *A Lover's Discourse* was Barthes' last teaching subject to make it into published book form (his seminar teaching having given rise to a number of texts and essays, from *s/z* onwards), and this suggests something important about his seminar experience: all the themes that he covered subsequently in his work at the Collège de France never made it into final published books. This was clearly something to do with the sociality of the seminar format at the EPHE, in contradistinction to the lecture format at the Collège (approximating to the 'laboratory' versus the lecture hall).

The key, 'social' link between *Roland Barthes by Roland Barthes* in 1975 and *A Lover's Discourse* in 1977 was Barthes' first set of lectures at the Collège de France, *Comment vivre ensemble* (How to Live Together).[27] As well as a fascinating literary account of being locked away, sheltered from the outside world (especially via Gide's extraordinary true story of a woman who lived permanently in her bedroom), *How to Live Together* was a deeply personal exploration of conviviality and solitude, especially for the researcher, writer and (and now-famous) lecturer:

Only writing is capable of picking out extreme subjectivity because only in writing there is a concord between the indirectness of the expression and the truth of the subject – concord that's impossible on the level of speech (and so impossible to achieve in a lecture course), because whatever our intentions speech is always both direct and theatrical. The book on the *Lover's Discourse* may not be as rich as the seminar, but I consider it to be more true.[28]

Typical of the post-'68 de-hierarchization and decentring of teaching since *s/z* and May '68, and of the influence of Zen Buddhism as a critique of mastery, Barthes was influenced not so much by hippies – indeed, we saw the opposite in his highly negative 1969 piece on hippies encountered in Morocco – but by the post-1968 move in France to the communes, to communal living. As the subtitle *Simulations romanesques de quelques situations quotidiennes* (Novelistic Simulations of Some Everyday Spaces) suggested, *How to Live Together* represented neither an attempt at erudition nor any proposal of practical guidelines. The novelistic (the novel without a story) set out the various 'scenes' of living in a group, in a kind of maquette (sketch, scale model or mock-up). Here Barthes' earlier interest in Fourier was mobilized, as he found pleasure in enumerating (as Fourier did, and as did Sade in more dubious ways).

Barthes thus alighted on an ideal integration of the individual into the social and the social into the individual, by investigating what Barthes called *délicatesse* – weakly translated as 'tact' in *The Neutral* – in which geographical space and social space became enmeshed in each other as a form of distance: what distance do we need between the self and society to instil sociability but to avoid alienation, to find solitude without exile? No concrete answer to this was supplied in *How to Live Together*, and Barthes abandoned his idea of exploring a utopia of living together at the end of the lectures. Nevertheless, it was Barthes' specialist knowledge of ancient Greek that allowed him to develop the idea and to coin its signifier: 'idiorrhythmy'. As a typical Barthesian neologism, 'idiorrhythmy' is, according to one critic, a 'principle that underlies an oriental sort of monachism in which everyone lives at his own rhythm'; and, ultimately, it was literature that could provide an idiorrhythmy.[29] Typically, the antithesis was used by Barthes to expound his idea. The opposite of idiorrhythmy would be a woman pushing her empty buggy with crying child in tow, in a graphic example of the 'dysrhythmic'.

In line with his own fascination with the 'Orient', Barthes stressed that idiorrhythmy came from the oriental – that is, anti-occidental – side of ancient Greek culture. But this was not the main point of his lectures. Overall, Barthes tried in *How to Live Together* to take solitude away from individualism and to see how it could be a 'collective experience', what he called a 'socialism of distances'. Here then appeared the significance of his central notion of *délicatesse* (in English, we might prefer 'fineness', or 'sensitivity', to 'tact'), which he found in the writings of the Marquis de Sade and which very much resembled the nvs (the refusal to seize hold) of *A Lover's Discourse*.[30] In the latter, 'the refusal to seize hold' of the loved one (*nvs, non-vouloir-saisir*) was a central way for the self in love, the loved self, not to be denied a true multidimensional existence; the *nvs* derived from his work on lovers' non-oppressive interaction could now become, more generally, a way for us all to live socially as individuals:

> Tact [*Délicatesse*] would mean: distance and respect, a relation that's in no way oppressive but at the same time where there's a real warmth of feeling. Its principle would be: not to direct the other, other people, not to manipulate them, to actively renounce images (the images we have of each other), to avoid anything that might feed the imaginary of the relation = Utopia in the strict sense, because a form of Sovereign Good.[31]

This *délicatesse*, argued Barthes, was impeded then by our creation of the image of the Other, and thus the visual (what is seen) was deemed suspicious, whereas touch, hearing and smell were valorized.

Another key aspect of idiorrhythmy was its active resistance to the 'event' and to the 'agitation of the 'Rhythmless'. In the dialectic of self and other, *How to Live Together* celebrated the 'smooth time' of solitude, 'subjected to a Rhythm'; this resultant idiorrhythmy could even be, in the long run, more dangerous than political revolts, argued Barthes, as solitude typically refused to participate in any re-stabilization of power. So in order to reflect the radical nature of the project, *How to Live Together*, as a new humanistic philosophy – both postcolonial and post-generic (and therefore utopian?) – was highly innovative in its presentation. The lectures (again) used the alphabetical as their structure in order to avoid both the 'dissertation' (with all the myths of mastery in this) on the one hand, and, on the other, the ruses of chance. In this way, *How to Live Together* was an example of culture rather than method (as differentiated by Deleuze and Nietzsche). Following the true meaning of 'encyclopaedia' – 'Research, not a Lecture' – Barthes' analysis was like a jigsaw we are invited to complete: 'I am the maker (the artisan) cutting out the pieces of wood. You're the players.'[32] However, despite the 'encyclopaedic' method he had developed for investigating how humans could live together, the idea seemed doomed to failure in practical terms, for a number of reasons.

Barthes' first reservation was that all forms of 'Acedia' were potentially fallible: a monk might have to return to normal life because he had lost faith in the meaning of solitude. Here Barthes arrived at his most startling, not to say 'depressing', view of the self (himself?):

no longer being capable of investing emotionally in other people, in Living-with-several-other people, yet at the same time being incapable of investing in solitude. Throwing it all away, but without even somewhere to throw it: waste without a waste-bin.[33]

Overall, Barthes seemed pessimistic about the possibility of a happy living together, and this was especially true, he suggested, when living together was part of a cause.[34] Though he held a utopian understanding of 'rule' versus 'law', Barthes saw that, largely, these communes do not – did not – work, hence a certain pessimism as to the viability of idiorrhythmy.

Not so much abandoning as leaving open his project of how to live together, Barthes moved, in his next lecture series between February and June 1978, onto a much more minimalist terrain by unearthing a negative figure from *Mythologies*, the *ni-ni* (neither-norism) of petit bourgeois criticism and ideology. But in 1977 he hoisted this petit bourgeois rhetorical figure into a positive search for a deconstruction of identity and identities. Far from being a support for narrow-minded notions of 'balance' and 'payment' – wittily associated by Barthes in 1957 with a refusal to commit, judge or take sides on the part of the bourgeois and petit bourgeois critic ('Neither-Nor criticism') – the 'neutral' now became a scandalous third space outside of the structuring binaries of modern alienated life, rather than an opting-out of deciding.[35] Thus *wou-wei* and Tao, as forms of Buddhist 'method', were shown also to be a form of oscillation; Barthes even responded in the lecture notes of *The Neutral* to letters and audience reactions with a precision: the neutral was 'only the desire for silence'.[36]

But a real *art de vivre* also emerged in this most utopian of lecture topics, in which tea in Japan was exemplified as a form of *délicatesse* – what Barthes called the 'minute', the fine detail, an idea that gestured to his book on Japan, *Empire of Signs*, in which the Japanese (meal) menu, in all its ritualistic meaning for the culture's signifying system, was analysed structurally for its social and cultural significance in Japan (and as a contrast with the de-ritualized Western way of eating).[37] This version of *délicatesse* – above all, an attention to detail, to 'nuance' – was 'oscillated' in the West into a form of 'social obscenity', against, in particular, the virility associated with a condemning of 'the delicate', the futile and the 'useless'; contrary to this, *délicatesse* vaunted a 'social errancy' in which the 'margins within the margin' were to be cherished.[38] If the margins were easily recuperated (fashion, on which Barthes had written a good deal, being a good example), then only the 'margins within the margin' could escape, but the *NVS* of *A Lover's Discourse* and *How to Live Together* also came to play its part.

Clearly the *NVS*'s refusal to seize hold was a key element of Barthes' analysis of love and of the general experience of being together for humans – a deeply social understanding of solitude, or rather, a deeply lonely version of sociality – and this became part of the *délicatesse* that he associated with the neutral: 'kinds of active protests or unexpected parrying against reduction, not of

Barthes in his room at home, June 1978.

the individual (it is not a matter of a philosophy of individualism) but of individuation (= the fragile moment of the individual)'.[39] The antithesis to the NVS's refusal to seize hold was the risk that the 'other's discourse (often well meaning, innocent) might reduce me to a case that fits an all-purpose explanation or classification in the most normal way', thereby leading to 'a breach of the principle of tact [délicatesse]'. From this stems the critique here, and elsewhere in Barthes' work, of the 'adjective', in opposition to 'sweetness' (douceur): 'Death in the child's arms' was the title that he would wish to give to this figure. This might be seen to clash with the 'fine' detail of the Marquis de Sade's love of dirty linen, unless we accept the other part of délicatesse's definition: 'a pleasure [jouissance] in analysis, a verbal operation that frustrates expectation (the laundry is dirty in order to be washed) and intimates that tact [délicatesse] is a perversion that plays with the useless (non-functional) detail.'[40] As well as preparing us for the 'punctum' of photography in Barthes' final essay Camera Lucida, this insignificant detail, crucial to délicatesse, emerged from its fundamental uselessness, its 'for-nothing' gratuitousness.

Thomas Clerc suggests, in the preface to The Neutral, that this lecture series showed Barthes now as the consummate 'artist-professor', rather than the self-dissolving essayist and teacher.[41] Indeed, Barthes' influential standing was now beyond doubt. Having befriended Antoine Compagnon, and supported his thesis on Montaigne, Barthes saw Compagnon return the favour by organizing a Colloque de Cerisy in June 1977 on Barthes. Sollers, Genette and Todorov (the 'middle' generation) all refused to participate in the week-long conference, and Robbe-Grillet apparently annoyed Barthes with his paper. But a new, younger generation at Cerisy, led by Compagnon, could be seen to be emerging as Barthes' new coterie: Evelyne Bachelier, Abdallah Bounfour, Hubert Damisch, François Flahault, Françoise Gaillard, Éric Marty, Patrick Mauriès, Jacques-Alain Miller

Barthes at home in June 1978, as ever with cigar in hand.

and Jean-Loup Rivière. Barthes acknowledged this new set of friends, colleagues and supporters at the conference.

Barthes' own paper – appropriately enough called 'The Image' – ended with a deep-felt appreciation of all of those friends and colleagues present.[42] But, typical of Barthes' obsession with language, it started with the idea that language was a 'battlefield' in society's larger *maché* (war), in which we found two unavoidable, categorical limits: *bêtise* (stupidity) and the *illisible* (unreadable). Barthes applied the first of these – stupidity – to the way that Marxism and psychoanalysis were, at first, 'counter-Stupidity', but 'once they take, there is stupidity'. The same thing happened with the image of the human subject: 'what I believe the other thinks of me' is just like frying chips – put a bit of potato into a frying pan and watch it being not destroyed, but 'hardened, caramelized, made crisp'. Other people's language makes him into an image, hence the *maché* for Barthes that is language.[43] Was this true of the image of Barthes too? Was that what he was saying? Was he hardened on the outside (we might think of Guérin, also known as Jean Paulhan, asking in 1955 if Barthes was a Marxist, of Camus' similar question, of *Mythologies*, of Picard, of May '68's structures not going out into the streets – that is, all the spats, all the moments when Barthes had felt 'fried' on the outside) and therefore soft on the inside? But crucially, even to refuse an image was itself to have an image: the degree zero was impossible even with one's own image. The only solution was *epoché*, the suspension – thwarting – of the image, which can only happen via a 'corruption' of words, by aesthetics, in literature; thus, in the discussion that followed his paper, especially with Robbe-Grillet, Barthes put forward this 'literary' solution to the image when he stated that he preferred that adjectives 'come to rest on him' (*se poser sur lui*), but not 'stick' (*coller*).[44]

Finally, Barthes proposed one more solution, which, aptly for us, was a personal-social one, and appropriately sourced from the ancient Greek of his undergraduate studies. *Acolouthia*, which was the 'transcendence of contradiction' that existed in society's *maché*, also meant to Barthes

> the retinue of friends who accompany me, guide me, to whom I entrust myself. I should like to designate by this word that rare field where ideas are steeped in affectivity, in which friends, by that retinue which accompanies your life, permit you to think, to write, to speak. These friends: I think for them, they think inside my head.[45]

What better way to thank those who had organized and come to the Cerisy conference on him? But also, what clearer statement, what more telling hymn to friendship, to the sociality of researching and writing, can we imagine? This was the 'Alpine Oxford' of his youth, of his illness, returning in triumph. But this was also the spirit of Barthes' writing, especially towards the end of his life, when his immense gratitude to his friends, to his colleagues and to his readership was increasingly signalled. Indeed, this deep friendship might be related to the power of the essay form. The fact that Barthes had 'worked' the seminar on the 'discourse of love' into a book, *A Lover's Discourse*, made his investment of self so different from the writer's journal.[46] In fact, the book version 'permitted a transcendence of the extreme particularity of its subjectivity'.[47] So writing (for publication), 'essayfying' his teaching, could perhaps be one way to get away from egotism, what Compagnon called *vouloir-écrire* (wanting to write). However, the writer's journal did have values of its own – at least in this period of his life.

As Barthes had to confront the extreme suffering and sudden solitude following his mother's death in 1977, the journal became a way of eradicating anguish by writing. His mother started her swift decline in July 1977, six months after Barthes' inaugural lecture at the Collège de France; one can only surmise that her pride in her son's extraordinary achievement made the pain of her death that much harder for him to bear.

7

Fame, Death and the 'Aristocratic' Self

I believe in an aristocracy of the sensitive, the considerate and the plucky.
They represent the true human condition, the one permanent victory
over cruelty and chaos.

E. M. Forster

Barthes' fame was undeniable by the mid-1970s.[1] The constant
media attention led to a parody of Barthes – *Le Roland-Barthes
sans peine* (Roland Barthes Made Easy, Burnier/Rambaud, 1978)
– which suggested, tongue-in-cheek, that there was a new French
language invented by Barthes that was being used throughout
French society. All of this sent up, in a rather suspicious, anti-
intellectual fashion, the theory that Barthes had seemingly
become a 'guru'.[2] Barthes' fame in 1977 was such that he appeared,
with the popular novelist Françoise Sagan, on the influential
television programme *Apostrophes* and its special edition 'Parlez-
nous d'amour' (Let's Talk About Love). He was also regularly
interviewed on French radio. As an illustration of the 'charivari'
(highly varied experiences) that Barthes had attributed to his life
in *Le Lexique de l'auteur* in 1973–4, he wrote articles during 1977
and 1978 in both *Vogue for Men* and *L'Humanité*, the Communist
Party daily in France! Barthes was also of those intellectuals in
the late 1970s keen to soften France's harsh laws on sexuality
and majority – he signed a high-profile letter in favour of the
release of three homosexual men from prison, and this solidarity

with homosexuals occurred even before the death of his mother, from whom he was reputedly keen to hide his own sexuality.[3]

The year 1977 was also the year when Barthes' political credibility on the left was tested. His acceptance to attend a dinner with the conservative French president Giscard d'Estaing (alongside other left-wing personalities such as Sollers, the radical lawyer Gisèle Halimi and the historian Emmanuel Le Roy Ladurie), held at the politician Edgar Faure's home, must have been seen as a betrayal by some. This was not helped by his seeming support for the *nouveau philosophe* Bernard-Henri Lévy's trenchant rejection of Marxism in 1977, and Barthes was one of the few leftists, alongside Sollers and Foucault, to engage with Lévy's critique of totalitarianism.[4] As we saw at the Colloque de Cerisy in Chapter Six, Barthes was also weary of the way that Marxism and psychoanalysis seemed to become 'stupid' languages once they had 'taken hold'. Indeed, the mid-1970s onwards saw a marked retrenchment of revolutionary and radical intellectuals in France, as Soviet and then Maoist ideologies were roundly exposed for the human abuses that their respective political systems were masking. There was clearly a new atmosphere, politically and intellectually in France, after 1976, especially with the arrival of the 'new' philosophers, who, former Maoist and Marxist *gauchistes* themselves during the 1968–75 period, had now swiftly recanted; in addition, some of Barthes' friendships in the late 1970s, such as with writer Renaud Camus, have not passed the political test of time.[5] It may be that this period of the late 1970s was not the best time to try to repeat the success of more than twenty years before in *Mythologies*; in 1979 Barthes' monthly chronicle in the centre-left weekly magazine *Le Nouvel observateur* – on a hugely diverse range of subjects, from the Nazi film-maker Leni Riefenstahl to the dancer Rudolf Nureyev, and from Mao and Tao to Superman – was not considered a success, and it finished after three months.[6]

Nevertheless, in the second half of the 1970s, Barthes felt that he had other subjects to research. If 1960s structuralism had been credited with the evacuation of the human subject from explanations of social change, the return to the 'self' in the next decade was to be an enduring and wide-ranging phase in Barthes' career. Coinciding with his accession to near-fame status in France, it also meant a greater freedom to write his essays. *The Pleasure of the Text* (1973) attempted to take literary culture away from oppositional politics – a sign of the struggle slowly waning in France – and Barthes began an extended examination of the image of the writer, in the person of Barthes, hence the use of the third person in *Roland Barthes by Roland Barthes* in an attempt to be objective about oneself. The interest in self and other, in the most acute of inter-subjective relations – love, or rather the language and personal politics of love – was then given literary, essayistic treatment in Barthes' best-selling book of his lifetime, *A Lover's Discourse: Fragments*.

Barthes also maintained his support of a writer mired in arguments in his collection of essays *Writer Sollers* (1979), which contained, among other ideas, a very perceptive understanding of how the images of people have replaced society's use of beliefs, for which 'Oscillation' (the title of the original essay on Sollers from 1978) was a critique of this image-dominated society. But two events in the same year marked and shaped the end of Barthes' career and the last years of his life: his appointment in 1977 to a chair in Literary Semiology at the prestigious Collège de France in Paris, and the death of his mother, also in 1977. The first of these events pushed Barthes into a new teaching function: no longer the hard-working seminar tutor, but the magisterial lecturer. This new way of working opened up other ways of writing and researching.

There is no doubt that the death of Barthes' mother in October 1977 knocked the stuffing out of him. Indeed, though announced (and subsequently published) as beginning in 1977, the lecture series at the Collège de France that he gave following his bereavement, *The Neutral*, was in fact delayed until February 1978. Many of the terms of the neutral that Barthes explored in this lecture series intimated this loss of appetite for life: 'Weariness', 'Sleep', 'Retreat', 'Fright', 'Apathy' and 'Anxiety' are all key terms in *The Neutral*. He also abruptly announced to the assembled audience that the lecture series would not (as previously) comprise any seminars, and this was indicative of the distance Barthes was feeling at this difficult time of mourning. And yet, typical of the oscillator that Barthes was, the exploration of the concept of the 'neutral' generated a whole new series of positive terms for his research and writing: 'Tact' (*délicatesse*), 'Intensities', 'Colour', '*Kairos*' and '*Wou-wei*' all testified to a certain 'will to live'. The dead-end of his previous lecture course, *How to Live Together*, had now been transformed into a fragile but operable stance within the neutral, to the extent that *The Neutral* is, today and even at the time, one of Barthes' most popular themes.[7]

Part of the interest in the neutral was its ability to undermine the numerous binaries that had guided Barthes' research since the discovery of Saussure in the 1950s and his use of semiology thereafter. Indeed, under the section 'Oscillation' in *The Neutral*, Barthes showed himself to be acutely aware of the way in which binaries, structural opposites, tended to obscure the 'nuance', the finer details in between.[8] Barthes had stumbled upon the nuances of life in his previous book, *A Lover's Discourse*, published just before his mother's death in 1977. Here he had underlined his *pharmakon* view of French vocabulary, in which language was presented as both illness and remedy and acutely felt in matters of love and amorous disappointment. Though this essay, typically built on short fragments, revealed few details of Barthes' own love-life, the concentration on the language of love, in all its splendour and treachery, allowed him to play out – literally to theatricalize – the situations by which he (like all of us) had found himself confronted by his loves and losses. At the end of *A Lover's Discourse*, having staged in language the endless games and ironies of being in love, Barthes came to a distinctly 'neutral' conclusion. He announced on

Barthes in 1977, soon after the death of his mother.

the last page that the NVS had to override any and all declarations of love; 'I love you' might have been running around in his head when contemplating a loved one, but it must remain 'imprisoned' behind his lips. In order to avoid oppressing the loved one, he must say 'silently', 'I hold back from loving you'.

This neutrality in one's love-life was but a prelude to a much wider refusal – albeit painted as positive – to oppress the Other. Indeed, by actively refusing to oppress the Other, Barthes was hoping, quite naturally, that others would not oppress him by attributing any one image (or any image at all) to him. Though the neutral becomes a convenient starting point for his own writing and research to start afresh in the wake of his mother's death, it was also a genuine part of his attempt to fight the 'image' that society gives us. Indeed, during this mid-1970s period, Barthes vaunted what he called, following Sartre, his *fuite en avant* (escape forwards): the *déclassé* (unclassified) intellectual self then searched for the notions of *perte* (loss) and the dissolution of self using the figure of the spiral as a sign that 'Roland Barthes' was a radically changing self. The lectures on 'The Neutral' thus provided the theoretical basis for this radical attempt at undermining the self's social Image.

In the section of *The Neutral* whose title, 'The Active of the Neutral', underlined its paradoxical *non*-passivity, Barthes defined the unclassifying neutral as something that 'denies uniqueness but recognizes the incomparable: the unique is shocking precisely in that it implies a comparison, a crushing under quantity; it implies singularity, even originality, which is to say competitiveness, agonistic values'. The neutral, by contrast, insisted upon the 'no ranking', upon Zen's 'bodily restraint', which is typical of *jiu-jitsu* (which, Barthes reminded, means 'the art of suppleness').[9] Barthes had worked extensively, in his previous lecture series on 'How to Live Together' and in his earlier essay on lovers' discourse, on relations with others, in both language and in real-life living together. All of these relations with the other came into conflict with human acts of classification. It was now in the 'Neutral' lectures that Barthes began to glimpse what the Marquis de Sade had referred to as *délicatesse*, the 'tact' required in maintaining the singularity of the self, the uniqueness of person, what he termed the 'aristocratic' notion of distinction in relation to the social *combinatoire*. The aristocratic, it must be stressed, needs to be understood not in the social or class sense, but as exception, as distinction, similar to the way in which Barthes, in 1962, had considered the nineteenth-century phenomenon of the dandy.[10] The 'aristocratic' self was now linked to the *délicatesse* of Japanese culture (especially in its food and in the 'lightness' of the haiku). Specificity now began to rub up against acts of classification; and *délicatesse* played a clear part in this singularization.

The notion of *délicatesse* was dependent on the ethics of *non-vouloir-saisir* (*NVS*), as described in *A Lover's Discourse* and the *How to Live Together* lecture series. These ways of not oppressing the Other (nor allowing others to oppress the self) were subsequently theorized in the lectures on the neutral. As well as citing examples in which the self loses its 'arrogance' (such as during Walter Benjamin's encounter with hashish in Marseille in 1932), Barthes tried to explain the importance of being 'neutral' in our relations with others. In the section 'Tact and Sociability', Barthes loosely defined *NVS* and *délicatesse* as 'kinds of active protests or unexpected parrying against reduction, not of the individual (it is not a matter of a philosophy of individualism) but of individuation'. The risk in any society, argued Barthes, was that 'others' discourse (often well meaning, innocent) reduces me to a case that fits an all-purpose explanation or classification in the most normal way'.[11]

The 'tact' that Barthes proposed as a way of undermining this 'reduction' of the self was to practise 'a kind of social obscene (the unclassifiable)', hence the (curious, unclassifiable?) example of the imprisoned Marquis de Sade being asked for sullied under-wear by the Marquise. Also, with typical Barthesian panache, he reminded the audience of the etymology of *delicatus* (effeminate, non-virile), exemplifying 'the useless, the futile . . . feminine' in the Japanese haiku, contiguous as these ephemeral short poems were with 'a kind of social errancy . . . margins within the margins', a uselessness in the social world of fashionability and usefulness:

> This amorous state 'unhooked' from the desire-to-possess
> (a [male or female] partner) can generate a whole complex
> of feelings-values that Japanese (notably with regard
> to haiku and Zen) call *sabi*: 'simplicity, naturalness,
> unconventionality, refinement, freedom, familiarity singularly
> tinged with aloofness and everyday commonness which is veiled
> exquisitely with the mist of transcendental inwardness'.[12]

This 'sweetness' of the self – 'the nonviolent refusal of reduction, the parrying of generality by inventive, unexpected, nonparadigmatizable behaviour, the elegant and discreet flight in the face of dogmatism' – presents a challenge to all human beings in their interaction with others, and represents the enduring importance of the Barthesian 'neutral' for any 'art of living' in contemporary society.[13]

However, it is important to stress that the 'neutral' stance that Barthes desired was also related to wider questions of society and politics. Barthes' 'neutral' in 1977 was a more sophisticated, even philosophical, exploration of the 'silence' he had adopted on political matters since his return from the 1974 *Tel Quel* visit to China, on which his only real comment was that he had 'no comment'. Thus neutrality was not so much an abdication as a principled (albeit highly nuanced) stance, in the face of a potentially hostile anti-Maoist French press and wider society.

Published posthumously, the three lecture series that Barthes gave at the Collège de France – *How to Live Together* in 1977 (2013), *The Neutral* in 1978 (2002) and *The Preparation of the Novel* in

1978–80 (2002) – as well as his 'inaugural lecture', all pointed to an opening up of new concerns in Barthes' thought, particularly in relation to utopias of the 'self'. This 'self' might be fluid, unclassifiable, 'aristocratic' and literary, but it was also the mourning self that came to dominate the last two years of Barthes' writing. First, in his seminal treatise on photography, *La Chambre Claire* (*Camera Lucida*, 1980), Barthes searched for his mother's presence or essence in photography, and while so doing supplied a stunning, if 'subjective', view of photography.[14] Second (but only published posthumously), his *Mourning Diary* (2009 [1978]) revealed a deeply alienated and lost 'self', and it has often been suggested that the minor traffic accident that befell Barthes in February 1980 as he left a lunch with future French president François Mitterrand was in itself not enough to end his life, but that his depression since his mother's death had left him with little will to live. It was no coincidence that another French writer, Marcel Proust, who was also pained by the death of his mother, became increasingly important in this final period of Barthes' life.

In *The Neutral* lecture series, Barthes described Proust losing his mother in 1905, leading to that obscure moment (epiphany?) in 1909 when the writing proper of *À la recherche du temps perdu* had started. A similar epiphany occurred when Barthes' mother died on 25 October 1977; this new life led to what he called, following Michelet (and before him, Dante), his *vita nova*. In *The Preparation of the Novel* lecture series, this was tantamount to creating, after the 'complete break of life', a new 'I'.[15] It involved, first, keeping a diary of his feelings towards his now recently deceased mother. Barthes had tried to keep a diary of his *Tel Quel* visit to China in 1974, and, before that, in Morocco in 1969, called *Incidents*. Both of these could be considered to have 'failed' as possible publications and were subsequently published only posthumously. Was this true of the *Mourning Diary*? Or was it too painful to publish, as if Barthes had taken his writing-for-nothing, writing-as-occupational-therapy to heart?

In the *Mourning Diary*, Barthes made some very stark and heart-felt admissions, clearly unable to find solace in the psychoanalytical notion of 'mourning', to which he preferred (a more Christian) 'suffering'. Now that his mother was dead, Barthes took up her habits, her way of keeping the apartment, and declared solemnly that he had now become her: 'Henceforth and forever I am my own mother', he declared in a parody of Michelet's famous comment (which we saw quoted by Barthes in 1942 in Chapter Two) that, as the writer of France's history, Michelet *was* his work.[16] As we have seen, this becoming Other (here, mother) was common in Barthes' decentring of self, in his 'thinking through others' (and others thinking 'through' him). But now he applied this idea to the most personal and intimate of his relations, and we will come back in a moment to his ultimate tribute to his mother when we see how he inscribed her into his final essay, *Camera Lucida*.

Just as he was only beginning to think about writing *Camera Lucida* in November 1977, Barthes took on his mother's other role, of 'looking after' his younger half-brother Michel Salzedo (although now in his forties). But crucially, as well as the deep pain and chagrin of loss, his mother's demise was a stark reminder of his own mortality, and it is here that a biographer's conundrum starts. If the death of his mother was the major changing point in Barthes' life, then, asks Marie Gil, how can we organize his life into a narrative when the major break comes at the very end of his own life (that is, less than three years before his own death)? Gil argues that the first part of Barthes' life 'as text' ended in 1977 with his mother's demise: after that, it was the *vita nova*.[17] Indeed, as Gil points out, Barthes might have led a dual life, a 'neuter' life – happy with his family affections, but anxious, lonely and bored in terms of friendship – but this neuter was what Gil calls the 'matrix of emptiness': the absence of the father, of social status as a war orphan, of money as a child, of completed studies thanks to tuberculosis, of a stable job, of qualifications needed.[18]

Unconsciously (that is, probably unbeknown to Barthes himself),
Barthes, she suggests, had to 'wait' for his mother's death before he
could 'consider' writing a novel. Up until then, his (semi-orphaned)
status had meant a 'lack' in relation to the absent father – the *nom
du père* (in Lacan's terms) being entirely absent in his family life –
which resulted in (was compensated by) an 'oscillation' that we have
witnessed across his career.[19] Up until 1977 Barthes could not write
a novel due to the three (seemingly essential) categories that would
repel him: 1) the 'smooth' and the 'continuous' nature of the prose;
2) the need for proper names; and, 3) the use of the third person.
All these requirements for a novel were compromised for Barthes,
but now 'released' from (half of) the family structure of 'lack' – and
himself not having been involved in any procreation – Barthes could
see, in the last phase of his career, a literary magnum opus of some
sort. (He even called the first set of lectures of *The Preparation of the
Novel* 'from life to work'.) Indeed, his self-acknowledged status as
un être pour rien (a being without offspring) was seen as analogous
to writing in its similarity to a social perversion.[20] The dualism that
was so prevalent in Barthes' career now disappeared following his
mother's death in 1977; for the last three years of his life, dualism
– oscillation included – was replaced in favour of the neuter, the
'immobility of essence', as part of Gil's metaphor of a photograph
developing across Barthes' life, but only fully visible after his
mother's death.[21]

In his last lectures at the Collège de France in 1979 and 1980,
The Preparation of the Novel lecture series, Barthes could see himself,
as the title suggests, putting himself into a position in which the
novel could be written. In *Camera Lucida* – *if* it was the novel he was
thinking about in *The Preparation of the Novel* lectures (and no other
'novel' has, so far, been found in his papers) – Barthes explored a
number of the 'preparations' on which he had been lecturing.[22]
As well as a direct reference to his mourning for his mother, in
which he hinted that it was necessary before the return of the

letter (or before being able to start writing again, with the pain of bereavement now enunciable), Barthes' lectures on *The Preparation of the Novel* contained numerous parallels and links to his final work on photography.

In the second year of *The Preparation of the Novel* lectures (1980), Barthes alighted on two types of book one might think of writing: on the one hand the big book – the magnum opus dreamed of by Mallarmé and by Proust – and on the other, the album, a form despised by Mallarmé.[23] Having discussed their relative merits – the former being, in Mallarmé's words, 'architectural and premeditated', 'total', 'sum' and 'pure'; and the latter being circumstantial, discontinuous, rhapsodic, diary-like, atonal and without cadence (in musical terms), and beholden to the 'spoken', and in which the notational leads to the 'deflated' nature of the contents – Barthes hesitated to choose between the two (it was only the 'preparation of the novel', after all). 'Suspended before me, like the two options of a difficult decision', he wrote in a manner reminiscent of his Taoist *wou-wei* strategy of 'refusing to choose'. To write a novel as if it were a (Mallarméan) book would be to hierarchize, transcendentally; to write it as an album would be to de-hierarchize, de-totalize, in a 'pure weaving of contingences'.[24] It would not take much to link this Album to *Camera Lucida*: its 'like that' status, its 'as it comes' approach was clearly linked to the *Tel* (Thus) of photography, to the 'incident' of the haiku – the fragment of writing in what Barthes called, following the German Romantics, *bariolage* (the motley) or, following the ancient Greeks, *poikilos* (the indistinct). Therefore, the album, this motley writing, was close to, able to deal with, the experience of the photographic image.[25] In this reckoning, *Camera Lucida*, Barthes' treatise on photography, was precisely this album that he was describing in his lectures in January 1980 (just as *Camera Lucida* was published). However – and hence Barthes' marked hesitation – to write *Camera Lucida* as an album would be to miss the Proustian moment that Barthes, having recently lost his mother, was keen to analyse, if not re-enact in spiral.

Indeed, the spiral was a useful figure for Barthes in the 1970s because it allowed him to revisit old themes in a new light:

> *The Spiral*: this form of time which is necessary to the move-ment of the dialectic may be a form of time for a whole life: he [Barthes himself, in the third person] began, as an adolescent, by having to undergo all of the literary *Doxa* which made the life of a writer into the original material for his/her work; then, he had to elaborate, practise the paradox to this *Doxa*, and liquidate biography; and it is only after this that he has been able to bring back the author *in a different place*, in the form of discontinuous traits, of biographemes: we revolve, in spiral, with the same object.[26]

Thus, all the while thinking of his own bereavement, Barthes underlined that Proust's tragic loss of his mother had been in 1905, but that the results of this loss – his starting to write his great novel – were then delayed until 1909.[27] If the irreplaceable nature of his mother was part of the 'Thus' (*Tels*) that Barthes saw in the photographic work of Richard Avedon, and in the inability to name the loved one other than by *Tel* (Thus) in *A Lover's Discourse*, then this would seem to push *Camera Lucida* close to being an album.[28] Then again, we must not ignore that Barthes, having completed the mourning process by 1980, underlined how it had led to 'acedia' – 'the inability to love (someone, other people, the world)' – and this surely suggests that he needed to write a novel that erred on the side of the book.[29] In the end, Barthes left the discussion as a dialectic of the two: the album could be put together with a 'Book in sight'. By the same token, the book, as 'ruin', could be read, consumed, quoted, pulled apart and eroded like a karst relief. Barthes says 'What lives in us of the book is the Album: the Album is the *germen*; the Book, however grandiose, is merely the *soma* [non-reproducing cell].'[30]

This helps explain the surprise – even confusion – that critics have experienced when considering Barthes' last book. On the one hand, *Camera Lucida* (subtitled *Reflections on Photography*) was an attempt at a phenomenology of photography – the 'noeme' of 'what-has-been', the subjective distinction between *punctum* and *studium*, and the *entelechia* (gesture towards the future) of a photograph were all discussed in the first half of *Camera Lucida*, the book part, we might say. However, what we do not know as we read the first part of the essay is that all these theories were generated by his search for his mother's presence in that winter garden photograph that he decided not to show us, for Part II of *Camera Lucida* abandons this 'architecture', in favour of a deeply personal search for his mother's essence in the photograph – of Henriette as a girl standing next to her brother in the winter garden at their mother's house in Chennevières-sur-Marne in 1898 – which Barthes described but never showed.[31] As Richard Stamelman has pointed out, in a perceptive chapter in his book on the poetry of loss, the 'camera lucida' is not a camera at all.[32] The English translation of the title of the book *Camera Lucida*, 'the name given to a technique of mimetic representation . . . [that] trace[s] the image of an object of perception' (to quote Stamelman), implied that in order for a photograph to become a 'camera lucida' – a Micheletian 'resurrection' of an absent loved one – the writer must inscribe the absent one via a presence-absence of describing and reacting subjectively to the (unshown) photograph.

Barthes was thus returning to his youthful interest in Jules Michelet and in the historian's aim to resurrect the masses of history, except that Barthes was now applying this to his mother. If, as Barthes (and Christian Metz) had argued, photography was a 'contact with death', Barthes would use his essay – an album and/or a book – to inscribe into permanence a life (his mother's), thereby continuing that oscillation (here, between photography's connections to life and to death) that we have seen across his life and writing career.[33] However, the one big difference was that this oscillation now had a dialectical outcome (which Barthes deemed to be undialectical, due to its unproductibility for a man who himself had produced no children of his own) – a reminder of his own death:

> The horror is this: nothing to say about the death of one whom I love most, nothing to say about her photograph, which I contemplate without ever being able to get to the heart of it, to transform it. The only 'thought' I can have is that at the end of this first death, my own death is inscribed; between the two, nothing more than waiting; I have no other resource than this *irony*: to speak of the 'nothing to say'.[34]

The 'nothing to say' – a suspension of judgement – had been a regular Barthesian strategy for maintaining a radical stance in the face of political 'engagement', at least since the enthusiasm for the theatre of Michel Vinaver in 1956, through the 'creative criticism' of the 1960s and into his writing on Japan and China and the Zen-inspired *wou-wei* of the 1970s.[35] But here, faced with the death of his mother, Barthes had to admit that the 'nothing-to-say' now offered a marked melancholy through which the viewer of a photograph of absence and loss – such as Henriette's portrait in the winter garden – could only glimpse his own death to come. He declares 'I . . . experience a micro-version of death (of parenthesis): I am truly a spectre.'[36]

Though published by Cahiers du Cinéma (with Seuil and Gallimard), *Camera Lucida* showed Barthes' deep thinking on photography as opposed to cinema, which went back to his work on Eisenstein in 1970, his earlier work on the text/image nexus, *Mythologies*, his commentary on Roger Pic's photographic record of Brechtian theatre and even to the very Proustian second half of his essay 'Visages et figures' (1953).[37] In this essay, it is quite clear that the denial of identity that he had seen film and photography operating on the shape of human faces – the way in which we adopt a facial pose of the film stars of the moment, while we are, memorially, unable to remember the face of a loved one other than 'framed' as if in a film – had its echo in *Camera Lucida* nearly thirty years later when Barthes regretted our inability to access the Other, what he called 'the impossible science of the unique being'. From this derives the significance of the 'Photo' of the Winter Garden (notice the capital letters) in which he could see his mother as young girl, as it seemed to provide him with a utopian solution.[38]

However, to reduce the contents of *The Preparation of the Novel* lecture series to the question of how he should write his post-mourning account of photography *Camera Lucida* would be to miss what is enduring and original about Barthes' final period of work. Indeed, in a lecture series concerned with how to start writing a novel, it is perhaps surprising that Barthes looked at key political themes for the late 1970s. These ideas related to a politics of the self in society, how the self operates in a complex social and political world; most interestingly, Barthes looked at utopian notions of this self. Indeed, it is interesting in the 'late' Barthes to note how textual concerns began to lead to real-life concerns. Having pointed to his own work in 1942 on Gide's *Journal* and to his assertion in 1966 that Proust's life was not reflected in *À la recherche du temps perdu*, but rather that the opposite was true ('it is his [Proust's] life that is the text of his work'), Barthes adopted the third person to exemplify how this had happened in his own life and work:

> For example, this year (1972–1973), he produces a particular text by instigating these sorts of collusions between very different meetings with people; he sees in succession different subjects emerging from contexts that are highly eclectic

and incompatible (going to a 'nightclub' after talks with a communist militant); this breaks up the monotonous law in the account of life, it produces a kind of textual clatter [charivari].[39]

This was perhaps, obliquely at least, the earliest statement of the key final theme in Barthes' 'life as text' – that is, the literary-inspired notion, from the Marquis de Sade, of *délicatesse*, translated somewhat unsatisfactorily as 'tact'. This example of life's charivari – or clash – of different worlds in Barthes' life (which mixed, incongruously enough, nightclub social life and communism) suggested not simply that Barthes was a social *passeur* who could slide (imperceptibly, subtly) between different worlds, but that the *passeur* was *déclassé*.[40] Though *déclassé* signifies 'demoted socially' (even 'drop-out'), in French it also means a release from all classificatory or taxonomic constraints. If we think back

Barthes with Michel Foucault, Pierre Boulez, Gilles Deleuze and others at IRCAM in Paris, 1978.

to the 'inorigin' of money theme in his 1970 essay *s/z* – the fortune
of the Lanty family was part of the mystery in Balzac's story – then
Barthes' comment in *Roland Barthes by Roland Barthes* on his being
déclassé could, in fact, be radically amphibological: 'Poverty made
him a *desocialised* child, but not déclassé'.[41] The *déclassé* could
indeed be part of *délicatesse* (it is nearly an anagram of it too!).
In his paper at the Cerisy conference in 1977, Barthes (implicitly)
linked *délicatesse* and the *déclassé* to democracy. The democratic
was not at all to be defined as 'the realisation of a stifling "gregarity",
but as "what should produce aristocratic souls"', suggested Barthes,
quoting a commentator of Spinoza.[42] The normal opposition of
democracy and aristocracy was thus broken down and collapsed,
but this relied upon the exclusion of elitism. Quoting Brecht
('Woe to the country which needs heroes'), Barthes argued that the
'contract' at least had the virtue of avoiding the elitism of heroism
and villainy. Barthes had already linked the Saussurean linguistic
contract with the social contract.[43] In the discussion at Cerisy in
1977, Barthes now made it clear that the (new) aristocratic soul in
his view was not an ancient Greek notion whereby there must be
slaves, but an attention to difference, a rejection of indifference.[44]

This realization undoubtedly prepared the way for his
utopian desire for a 'science of the unique being' in *Camera
Lucida*. In other words, the experience of mourning his mother
helped to generate profound insights not just on photography,
but on the generality of the individual. This generality of the
individual relied on the *délicatesse* that Barthes had spent much
of the 1970s theorizing. In this sense, the call by Barthes for an
aristocracy of the self was far removed from the 'sovereignty' of the
self claimed by Georges Bataille; it was not a radical individuality,
but the 'socialism of distances' that he had explored in the *How
to Live Together* lectures. What would permit this 'living together'
that did not involve any oppression of the Other – of others – was
a world in which nobody was determined by any social class

Inaugural Lecture at the Collège de France, Paris, 1977.

position. The *déclassé* was a person who, like all others, was no longer beholden to a social origin. This was so typical of Barthes' iconoclasm, of his attention to binary oppositions and to their potential overcoming and collapsing. Indeed, Barthes was so often re-ordering opposites that we seem to have, when reading his work, so very few left standing, except for the 'value' of literature.

If 1977 saw a critique of Marxist radical thought, Barthes' short-lived *dérive* (slide) towards the Right was brought to an abrupt end by the prospect of France's first socialist president under the Fifth Republic set up by General de Gaulle back in 1958. Invited by Jack Lang to dine on 25 February 1980 with the *premier secrétaire* of the Parti Socialiste, François Mitterrand (only a year or so before the 'historic' election that led to him becoming president of France), Barthes emerged from the lunch, reached the rue St Jacques and, without seeing the laundry van approaching, was swiftly knocked over, right outside the Collège de France on rue des Écoles.[45] Following a month in hospital – Barthes was no doubt used to this medicalized world (having spent four of his early adult years in the sanatorium with tuberculosis) – he died on 26 March 1980 of a 'nosocomial infection' at the relatively young age of 64. The suggestion was that the injury was not enough to cause his death; a lack of will to live might well have been.

Conclusion:
'Barthes is Not a Barthesian'

Barthes is firmly part of the French tradition of essayists that Montaigne, Rousseau, Gide and even Michelet, and for whom the self is constantly the vessel through which writing connects with the world. He might be placed in a much wider tradition of moralists (Nietzsche, Sartre and even Lacan and Lévi-Strauss) who want to explain, philosophically, how we behave as humans. Barthes' work is characterized nevertheless by a highly original critique of self and personality, understood as individuated by an alienated world, in which the self as social being was thoroughly investigated. One might object that in *Camera Lucida*, the final essay of his career, Barthes seemed to be saying that only the unique, the singular (his mother), mattered, making Barthes, in the final instance, into a deeply *a*social theorist. But isn't that the deep Hegelian paradox at the heart of human society? His singularity might not be ours (that is, individually). And yet, in the generality of our particular situation, everyone has a mother, and we are all stuck with the cruel conjugation of love with death. It is for this reason that Barthes' own 'mana' word was almost certainly 'writing' (*écriture*): 'writing is an act of historical solidarity', he wrote at one end of his career, and this became 'one needs a loving response when one writes' at the other end.[1] Are they *that* different?

All that we have said about 'Barthes' could be termed 'fictions', as Marie Gil has warned us in relation to the 'factual' in a writer's inscription of his life into his writing. Indeed, Gil comes close to

'La Maison Carboué', Barthes' home in Urt, a village near Bayonne, in Gascony, France.

saying that Barthes was a fictional essayist – not a novelist, nor a purveyor of fiction, but a *romanesquier* who inscribed himself into the fiction of all writing. This is certainly plausible for the 'late' Barthes, but less so for the earlier Barthes. Indeed, this shift might suggest a narrative of his life as writer. The 'late' Barthes seemed to 'dramatize' the self, in a way that had been largely absent in his more youthful writing. But, in educational terms, the 'excluded' Barthes of the 1930s–'50s had established, by the early 1970s, the 'luxury' of inscribing and of examining the self in the cold, objective and even scientific world of the seminar room or lecture theatre. Indeed, Barthes worked for half of his writing life in an academic institution (the EPHE) that benefited from the luxury of not needing to give out qualifications; the sociology of Barthes' writing therefore amounts to a type of *essayisme institutionnalisé* (essay writing in academia).

So the (structuralist) hoist is perhaps there to complement the 'oscillation', the binary 'two sides' to Barthes' world. The more he classified, reclassified and over-classified – including himself – the more he created the opportunity, the challenge to *de*classify (or un-classify) through his use of language:

> Language is legislation, speech is its code. We do not see the power which is in speech because we forget that all speech is classification, and that all classifications are oppressive.[2]

And yet, as we have seen, Barthes' fascination with Saussure, with semiology and linguistics, was tightly related to the classifications – taxonomy – of communicative and social phenomena. Indeed, one way around this classificatory oppression for Barthes was his trademark use of the artifice of the alphabetical list, as a way of pointing to the arbitrary nature of classifications.

This contradiction raises a key question for a biography of Barthes. Barthes was always keen to 'deconstruct a totality'.[3] So how might this deconstruction in Barthes' writing fit with Gil's use of psychoanalysis as a 'total' approach to Barthes' biography? Is there not a danger that Gil's apportioning to Barthes the figure of 'oscillator' might contradict his marked attempts to undermine 'the desire to possess' another human being, that her biography locks Barthes into a box or a hole? It might be then that, rather than an 'oscillator', it is Houdini who provides a better image for Barthes, as this implies, in his attempts to break out from institutional and societal closure and control, a notion of creativity.[4] Indeed, following our discussion of Barthes' *délicatesse*, we might ask how the 'aristocratic' relates to the social self. Is it the figure of the 'amateur', the person who operates through the love of what he does, but is always outside, critical and suspicious, of the institutional control of being 'professional' or being 'master' of what one does? And what might it mean to analyse the 'social' Barthes as one who was suspicious above all of 'classification'?

In a recent analysis of Barthes' philosophical approach, Jean-Claude Milner suggests that Marx and ideological critique were so entrenched in Barthesian criticism, writing and thought that the (relatively) sudden disappearance of Marx and Marxian categories from his work in the last period of Barthes' life was less to do with any move away from radical materialist utopias and critiques, than with a wholesale (albeit implicit) assumption of them. Milner quotes a private comment by the lifelong friend of Barthes and his editor at Seuil, François Wahl, who insisted, from start to finish, that Barthes' life rested on a *soubassement marxiste* (Marxist underpinning).[5] For Marx, capitalism is a social relation, and it is the height of fetishism to identify possession of any goods with capital. If both capital and language are social relations, then language must play a significant role in these alienated social relations. Does this attribution of Marxian categories to the fundamentals of Barthes' work mean that we have to perform the critique of psychoanalysis that is largely absent from Barthes' work? One way out of this conundrum is to see Barthes as a social psychologist (rather than a psychoanalyst). Indeed, one great historical example of a politicized social-psychology comes in Marx's brilliant dictum 'All that I know is that I am not a Marxist.' This dictum presents a stunningly open dialectic in one sense: it gestures generously to the future. But it is dialectical, in another sense: in its relation to the time of Marx's own life, with history. Thus Barthes followed this social psychology (and not social psychoanalysis, since this is an oxymoron, concerned only with the individual, albeit in all of its contradictions), and brought it up to date with a structural understanding of self and society and of self in society. It is tempting, therefore, to say, with all the distance and dissolution of self and in a parody of Marx's *mot*, that 'Barthes is not a Barthesian.'

References

Introduction

1 Éric Marty, 'La Vie posthume de Roland Barthes', in *Barthes après Barthes: une actualité en questions*, ed. C. Coquio and R. Salado (Pau, 1993).
2 See, for example, 'One Always Fails in Speaking of What One Loves', which is Barthes' last (unfinished) essay, in Roland Barthes, *The Rustle of Language*, trans. Richard Howard (Oxford, 1986), pp. 296–305, or his final book, *Camera Lucida* (Paris, 1980).
3 Alain Robbe-Grillet, *Why I Love Barthes* (Cambridge, 2011), p. 26.
4 J.-L. Jeannelle, 'Barthes ne se laisse pas faire', *Le Monde des livres* (9 March 2012), p. 9.
5 Marie Gil, *Roland Barthes: Au lieu de la vie* (Paris, 2012), p. 21; Gil's biography has been swiftly superseded by the authorized biography by Tiphaine Samoyault (Paris, 2015), whose publication has been timed to coincide with the centenary of his birth.
6 Roland Barthes, *Oeuvres complètes*, ed. Éric Marty (Paris, 2002), vol. III, p. 1025.
7 G. Mounin, *Introduction à la sémiologie* (Paris, 1970), p. 65.
8 Octavio Paz, untitled prose poem, in *Early Poems, 1935–1955*, trans. Muriel Rukeyser (New York, 1973), p. 61.
9 Roland Barthes, 'On Gide and His *Journal*', in *A Barthes Reader*, ed. Susan Sontag (London and New York, 1982), p. 15.
10 Roland Barthes, *Image-Music-Text*, trans. Stephen Heath (Glasgow, 1977), pp. 142–8.
11 In *Roland Barthes et l'étymologie*, Cécile Hanania defines *maché* as a 'contradictory presentation of the subject with its self'; see Cécile Hanania, *Roland Barthes et l'étymologie* (Brussels, 2010), p. 117.

1 War Orphan

1 See Patrizia Lombardo, *The Three Paradoxes of Roland Barthes* (Athens, GA, 1989).

2 Roland Barthes, *Oeuvres complètes*, ed. Éric Marty (Paris, 2002), vol. IV, p. 899. In a very late interview in January 1980 (*OC*, V, 947), Barthes even underlines how he has nostalgia for his grandparents' era of the late nineteenth century, for it was through them that he was acculturated as a small child. From this also stems his fascination with Proust's generation, including photographs of Proust's family and social milieu – see Roland Barthes, 'Proust and Photography', in *The Preparation of the Novel: Lecture Courses and Seminars at the Collège de France (1978–1980)*, trans. Kate Briggs (New York, 2011), pp. 305–75.

3 Roland Barthes, *Roland Barthes by Roland Barthes*, trans. Richard Howard (London, 1977), p. 27. See the 1976 radio interview with Barthes, 'L'Autoportrait', cited by Marie Gil, *Roland Barthes: Au lieu de la vie* (Paris, 2012), p. 59.

4 Barthes, *Roland Barthes by Roland Barthes*, pp. 60–61.

5 Gil, *Roland Barthes: Au lieu de la vie*, p. 35. Barthes even has a view, in later life, that his November birth date is barely in 1915, but also that 1915 is an 'anodine' year in which to be born, 'lost' as it is in the midst of the Great War, when no one famous dies; and, saying that he knows nobody born in this exact period, Barthes even wonders whether he was the only person of his specific age. See Roland Barthes, *Le Lexique de l'auteur: Séminaire à l'École pratique des hautes études, 1973–1974* (Paris, 2010), p. 318.

6 This 50-minute television interview with Jean-José Marchand (as part of the *Archives du xxe siècle*) was published in part in *Tel Quel*, XLVII (1971) as 'Réponses' (*OC*, III, 1023–44) and translated as 'Responses: Interview with *Tel Quel*', trans. Vérène Grieshaber, in *The Tel Quel Reader*, ed. Patrick ffrench and Roland-François Lack (London, 1998), pp. 249–67. It was recorded between November 1970 and May 1971, made by Philippe Colin and shown on French television in 1988.

7 Left-handed children were physically encouraged, up until recently, to 'repair' their left-handedness, something that Barthes considered a 'discreet' form of social oppression and exclusion. See Barthes, *Roland Barthes by Roland Barthes*, p. 98.

8   Louis-Jean Calvet, *Roland Barthes: A Biography* (London, 1994), p. 22. Calvet lists the school prizes that Barthes won in 1931 at the age of sixteen, in geography, history, French composition, Latin–French translations, recital and even physical education.

9   *En marge du 'Criton'* was finally published in *L'Arc*, LVI (1974), pp. 3–7; this was a special number on Barthes.

10 Michel Jarrety, *Paul Valéry* (Paris, 2008), cited in Gil, *Roland Barthes*, p. 101.

11 Roland Barthes, 'The Bourgeois Art of Song', in *The Eiffel Tower and Other Mythologies*, trans. Richard Howard (New York, 1979), pp. 119–22.

12 'En Grèce' was published in the sanatorium journal, *Existences*, in 1944; see *oc*, I, 68–74.

13 Roland Barthes, 'Culture et tragédie', in *oc*, I, 29–32.

14 Interestingly, André Salzedo's wife, Maggie Salcedo, who (slightly) changed her name after their divorce, was a sculptor, precisely the vocation that Michel Salzedo would go on to fulfil.

15 One element in the critique of the factual, in Barthes' lifetime and intellectual milieu, is the insistence by psychoanalysis, specifically Jacques Lacan's structuralist version, that the final signified of the human psyche, around which all the chains of signifiers revolve, is 'lack', emptiness, the 'void'; see Roland Barthes, 'Une problématique du sens' [1970] in *oc*, III, 517.

16 This is to the extent that one could, conceivably, attempt to write Barthes' life 'backwards', starting from this organizational moment that is his mother's death. We will see, in Chapter Seven, how Barthes' own writing post-1977 reflects and encourages this backwards looking.

17 In his very final lecture series in 1980, *The Preparation of the Novel*, Barthes would claim, in a very tongue-in-cheek manner, that his 'illness', if one were using a 'cheap' form of psychoanalysis, was a way of avoiding 'a distressing familial, then national, situation'; see Roland Barthes, *The Preparation of the Novel* (New York, 2011), p. 223.

2   Tubard

1   Roland Barthes, *Roland Barthes by Roland Barthes*, trans. Richard Howard (London, 1977), p. 35.

2 This phrase, attributed to Barthes by Marie Gil, *Roland Barthes: Au lieu de la vie* (Paris, 2012), p. 137, appeared in an article in the sanatorium's journal *Existences* under the pseudonym Émile Ripert.

3 Ibid., p. 146.

4 Ibid., p. 150.

5 Roland Barthes, *Oeuvres complètes,* ed. Éric Marty (Paris, 2002), vol. I, pp. 57–67 and 75–9.

6 See Barthes' quotation of Roger Laporte: 'A *pure* reading which does not call for *another writing* is incomprehensible to me', in Roland Barthes, 'On Reading' [1975], in *The Rustle of Language*, trans. Richard Howard (Oxford, 1986), p. 41.

7 Barthes, *Roland Barthes by Roland Barthes*, p. 61.

8 Two articles written and published in this period might seem to stand outside of this growing politicization: first, Barthes' piece for the catalogue on artist Dominique Marty (*oc*, I, 87–8); secondly, his review of two exhibitions, one of Marcel Gromaire and Jean Lurçat, and the other of Alexander Calder, published in *France-Asie* in January 1947 (*oc*, I, 91–5). Sartre had written an essay for the catalogue of Calder's exhibition of 1946 in Paris (and which Barthes mentions in his piece).

9 Apparently, there is an early version of the 'Degree Zero' thesis, written in 1946, but which never appeared; see Gil, *Roland Barthes: Au lieu de la vie*, p. 166.

10 This is the basis of a preface of 1958 on Voltaire in Roland Barthes, *Critical Essays*, trans. Richard Howard (Evanston, IL, 1972), pp. 83–9.

11 Louis-Jean Calvet, *Roland Barthes: A Biography* (London, 1994), p. 88.

12 In 1979 Barthes worried that his posterity would not earn enough to support Michel in Paris; he wrote in *Mourning Diary*, 'I live without any concern for posterity, no desire to be read later on (except financially, for M[ichel]'); see Roland Barthes, *Mourning Diary: October 26, 1977–September 15, 1979*, trans. Richard Howard (London, 2010), p. 234.

13 See Marie Gil, *Roland Barthes. Au lieu de la vie*, pp. 167 and 175.

14 *oc*, I, 132–4.

15 *oc*, I, 141–62.

16 *oc*, I, 163–5 and 229–33.

17 See, for example, *oc*, I, 101.

18 See Roland Barthes, 'On Gide and his Journal', in *A Barthes Reader*, ed. Susan Sontag (New York, 1982), p. 12.

19   *OC*, I, 109–23.

20   *OC*, I, 268–79, 548–54.

21   Roland Barthes, *Writing Degree Zero,* trans. Annette Lavers and Colin Smith (London, 1967), p. 7.

22   Barthes, *Roland Barthes by Roland Barthes*, p. 26.

3 Marxism, Popular Theatre and the New Novel

1   Published in the February 1953 number of *Esprit*; see Roland Barthes, *Oeuvres complètes*, ed. Éric Marty (Paris, 2002), vol. I, pp. 234–44.

2   *OC*, I, 245–52.

3   In *Théâtre populaire, 1953–1964: Histoire d'une revue engagée* (Paris, 1998), Marco Consolini considers that this *revue engagée* has now become 'mythical' in the history of post-war radical theatre.

4   *OC*, I, 458–60, 524–6, 578–80.

5   *OC*, I, 515–16.

6   Roland Barthes, 'Literal Literature', in *Critical Essays*, trans. Richard Howard (Evanston, IL, 1972), p. 58.

7   In one editorial, Barthes even wrote 'we vomit up bourgeois theatre' (*OC*, I, 459).

8   The play by Planchon was produced under the title *Les Coréens* and reviewed favourably by Barthes in 1956 (*OC*, I, 666–7).

9   Barthes' commentary is translated in part in *Tulane Drama Review*, XII/1 (1967) by Hella Freud Bernays.

10   Barthes' 'manifesto' of 1956 for Brecht's epic theatre, 'The Tasks of Brechtian Criticism', is included in the anthology *Marxist Literary Theory*, ed. Terry Eagleton and Drew Milne (Oxford, 1996), pp. 136–40.

11   *OC*, I, 540–7, 573–4.

12   *OC*, I, 596–7 and 599–604. According to Tiphaine Samoyault, Barthes was invited by Sartre, following his support for Sartre's play, to become theatre critic for the *Temps modernes* journal, but Barthes declined due to work pressure; see Tiphaine Samoyault, *Roland Barthes* (Paris, 2015), pp. 327–8.

13   Roland Barthes, 'Ornamental Cookery', in *Mythologies*, trans. Annette Lavers (London, 1993; revd edn 2009), pp. 89–92.

14   Roland Barthes, 'The Man in the Street on Strike', in *The Eiffel Tower*

and Other Mythologies, trans. Richard Howard (New York, 1979), pp. 99–102.

15 Roland Barthes, 'Myth Today', in *A Barthes Reader*, ed. Susan Sontag (New York, 1982), p. 101.

16 Guy Debord, *Society of the Spectacle* (London, 1977); Michael Kelly, 'Demystification: A Dialogue between Barthes and Lefebvre', *Yale French Studies*, XCVIII (2000), pp. 79–94.

17 Roland Barthes, 'Myth Today', in *A Barthes Reader*, p. 110.

18 Jean-Claude Milner, *Le Pas philosophique de Roland Barthes* (Paris, 2003), p. 54.

19 It was Violette Morin who introduced Barthes to the philosopher Vladimir Jankélévitch, with whom he shared a passion for piano duets.

20 *OC*, I, 974–6.

21 Roland Barthes, 'Authors and Writers', in *Critical Essays*, pp. 143–50. For these essays, see, respectively, Barthes, *Critical Essays*, pp. 110–15; Roland Barthes, *The Language of Fashion,* trans. Andy Stafford (Oxford and Sydney, 2006), pp. 59–64; *A Barthes Reader*, pp. 236–50; Roland Barthes, *Image-Music-Text*, trans. Stephen Heath (Glasgow, 1977), pp. 32–51; *A Barthes Reader*, pp. 218–35.

4 From Semiology to Structuralism

1 See Louis Althusser, '*Piccolo teatro*: Bertolazzi and Brecht: Notes on a Materialist Theatre' [1962], in *For Marx*, trans. Ben Brewster (London, 1969), pp. 129–51.

2 Roland Barthes, *Oeuvres complètes,* ed. Éric Marty (Paris, 2002), vol. I, pp. 234–42.

3 *OC*, I, 1039–56.

4 For an analysis of the film, see Scott MacKenzie, 'The Missing Mythology: Barthes in Québec', *Canadian Journal of Film Studies*, VI/2 (Fall 1997), pp. 63–74, www.filmstudies.ca/journal, accessed 15 July 2014.

5 However, according to Marie Gil, *Roland Barthes: Au lieu de la vie* (Paris, 2012), pp. 238–9, once he had completed a draft in 1961 (having worked all of summer 1960 on it in Hendaye), Barthes offered a version of his work on written fashion to Lévi-Strauss to read. This was, most

likely, the 'early' preface to his 1967 essay *The Fashion System*; see Roland Barthes, *The Language of Fashion*, trans. Andy Stafford (Oxford and Sydney, 2006), pp. 70–85. There was, however, no reply from the anthropologist, indicative perhaps of the one-way direction of their 'friendship'.

6 Roland Barthes, 'Kafka's Reply', in *Critical Essays*, trans. Richard Howard (Evanston, IL, 1972), pp. 133–8. See A. Green, 'Les *Mythologies* de Roland Barthes et la psychopathologie', *Critique*, CXXXII (1958), pp. 105–13.

7 Gérard Genette, *Bardadrac* (Paris, 2006).

8 Roland Barthes, *Le Lexique de l'auteur: Séminaire à l'École pratique des hautes études, 1973–1974* (Paris, 2010), pp. 276–7.

9 Georges Morin, 'La fin d'un commencement', in *Arguments, 1956–1962*, 2 vols (facs edn, Toulouse, 1983), vol. II, pp. 123–6 (p. 125). Morin might also have added that he and Barthes had recently launched a new – albeit 'institutionalized' – journal, called *Communications*.

10 See 'The Point about Robbe-Grillet?', in Barthes, *Critical Essays*, pp. 197–204.

11 See 'Authors and Writers', in Barthes, *Critical Essays*, pp. 143–50.

12 Ibid., pp. 145–6. Barthes' reading of Louis Hjelmslev's treatise on language played an important part in this, since *Prolégomènes à une théorie du langage* (Copenhagen, 1943; Paris, 1968) argues that science is a formal research that is intransitive.

13 Roland Barthes, *The Rustle of Language*, trans. Richard Howard (Oxford, 1986), pp. 11–19.

14 See 'Authors and Writers', in Barthes, *Critical Essays*, p. 150.

15 'Why I Love Benveniste', in *The Rustle of Language*, pp. 162–7. On this, see Philippe Maniglier, *La vie énigmatique des signes: Saussure et la naissance du structuralisme* (Paris, 2006).

16 (My emphasis); *Elements of Semiology*, trans. Annette Lavers and Colin Smith (London, 1967), p. 14.

17 See Roland Barthes, *The Semiotic Challenge*, trans. Richard Howard (Oxford, 1987), pp. 11–94.

18 See Barthes, 'Introduction to the Structural Analysis of Narratives', in *A Barthes Reader*, ed. Susan Sontag (New York, 1982), pp. 251–95.

19 Preface to Barthes, *Critical Essays*, p. xii.

20 See Barthes, 'Literature and Signification', in *Critical Essays*, p. 275.

21 Interestingly, Lucien Goldmann's *Racine* had been first published by L'Arche in 1956, precisely when Barthes was one of its literary consultants.

22 Roland Barthes, *On Racine*, trans. Richard Howard (Berkeley and Los Angeles, CA, 1992), pp. 151–72.

23 Raymond Picard, *Nouvelle critique ou nouvelle imposture?* (Paris, 1965; trans. Washington, DC, 1967, by Frank Towne).

24 Roland Barthes, *The Grain of the Voice: Interviews, 1962–1980*, trans. Linda Coverdale (New York, 1985), p. 41.

25 According to Gil, in *Roland Barthes: Au lieu de la vie*, p. 267, *On Racine* was written during one of Barthes' amorous difficulties, the 'Crise Olivier' of 1963; similarly, in *The Preparation of the Novel*, Barthes pointed out that as he was writing the *Mythologies* – between 1952 and 1956 – he was going through an 'intense crisis' in his personal life, leaving us to wonder whether this was related to Bernard Dort; see Roland Barthes, *The Preparation of the Novel: Lecture Courses and Seminars at the Collège de France (1978–1980)*, trans. Kate Briggs (New York, 2011), p. 245.

26 Jean-Paul Weber, *Néo-critique et paléo-critique, ou Contre Picard* (Paris, 1966), p. 15; Weber mentioned Barthes only once, despite acknowledging that Picard's attack was mainly against Barthes and his *On Racine*.

27 Roland Barthes, *Criticism and Truth*, trans. Katrine Pilcher Keuneman (London, 1987), p. 38.

28 Ibid., p. 12.

29 Ibid.; Barthes, *The Grain of the Voice*, p. 41.

30 Sontag, *A Barthes Reader*, pp. 236–50.

31 Barthes, *Critical Essays*, p. 157.

32 Ibid., pp. 149–50.

33 Ibid., pp. 163–70.

5 May '68

1 Cited in Edgar Faure, *L'Éducation nationale et la participation* (Paris, 1968), p. 12; Roland Barthes, *Oeuvres complètes*, ed. Éric Marty (Paris, 2002), vol. III, pp. 695–6.

2   See Marie Gil, *Roland Barthes. Au lieu de la vie* (Paris, 2012), pp. 322–3.

3   Roland Barthes, 'The Refusal to Inherit', in *Writer Sollers*, trans. Philip Thody (London, 1987), p. 69.

4   *OC*, III, 1005.

5   Catherine Backès-Clément reported that after a long student meeting, it was decided that 'Structures do not go into the street', the phrase being attributed to Barthes, and so a poster appeared the next day saying 'Barthes says: structures do not come out onto the streets. We say: neither does Barthes'; see Gil, *Roland Barthes: Au lieu de la vie*, p. 317.

6   See the 'Supplément exceptionnel' of *L'Express* (3 June 1968), p. 13, which had been delayed by the strikes and occupations.

7   *L'Express* (17–23 June 1968), p. 36.

8   Roland Barthes, *The Rustle of Language*, trans. Richard Howard (Oxford, 1986), pp. 149–54.

9   *OC*, IV, 475–6.

10 GET was the Groupe d'études théoriques. The published version of the seminars, *Théorie d'ensemble* (Paris, 1968) includes, as well as pieces by Derrida and Foucault, Barthes' rather curious re-reading of his own 1965 review of Philippe Sollers's novel *Drame* (pp. 27–42; republished in *Writer Sollers*); see also P. ffrench and R.-F. Lack, eds, *The Tel Quel Reader* (London, 1998).

11 Roland Barthes, *'Sarrasine' de Balzac: Séminaires à l'École pratique des hautes études (1967–1968 et 1968–1969)* (Paris, 2011); see especially the seminar of 21 November 1968, pp. 315–29.

12 Roland Barthes, 'From Science to Literature', in *The Rustle of Language*, pp. 3–10.

13 Unfortunately, this seminar is yet to be published, but it is available in the Bibliothèque nationale in Paris (see, in Barthes' archive, NAF 28630 *La Linguistique du discours*); see also Roland Barthes, 'The Discourse of History', in *The Rustle of Language*, pp. 127–40. Interestingly, as part of the invitations to the seminar that Barthes offers, there is a paper, in 1966, on the Portuguese writer Fernando Pessoa by José Augusto Seabra, providing another source for Barthes' ideas in the 1970s of the 'self as literary'.

14 The 'Old Rhetoric' was not published until 1970; see Roland Barthes, *The Semiotic Challenge*, trans. Richard Howard (Oxford, 1987), pp. 11–

94; Roland Barthes, *The Grain of the Voice: Interviews, 1962–1980*, trans. Linda Coverdale (New York, 1985), pp. 109–12.

15 Roland Barthes, *Image-Music-Text*, trans. Stephen Heath (Glasgow, 1977), pp. 142–8. In his critique of those who read 'Death of the Author' literally, J.-C. Carlier argues that it is more like a Menippean satire that is both pedantic and anti-pedantic; see J.-C. Carlier, 'Roland Barthes' Resurrection of the Author and Redemption of Biography', *Cambridge Quarterly*, XXIX/4 (2000), pp. 386–93 (pp. 388–9).

16 The rivalry between Goldmann and Barthes, colleagues at the EPHE, was despite (or perhaps because of) Goldmann's supervisory role in relation to Julia Kristeva's PhD thesis; interestingly, her PhD viva voce was held right in the middle of May '68, with both Barthes and Goldmann present.

17 See Jacques Lacan, *Écrits: A Selection*, trans. Alan Sheridan (London, 1977); Jacques Derrida, *Writing and Difference*, trans. Alan Bass (London and Chicago, 1978); and Jacques Derrida, *Of Grammatology*, trans. Gayatri Spivak (Baltimore, MD, 1977).

18 Barthes, *The Rustle of Language*, pp. 141–8.

19 Barthes, *The Fashion System*, trans. Matthew Ward and Richard Howard (London, 1985), pp. ix–x.

20 For a wide-ranging analysis of May '68 by French theorists from the time, see Charles Posner, ed., *Reflections on the Revolution in France: 1968* (London, 1970).

21 See François Dosse, Chapter Ten in *History of Structuralism*, vol. II: *The Sign Sets, 1967–present*, trans. Deborah Glassman (Minneapolis, MN, 1998).

22 On Marx as an early structuralist, see Maurice Godelier, 'System, Structure and Contradiction in *Das Kapital*' [1966], trans. Philip Brew, in *Structuralism: A Reader*, ed. M. Lane (London, 1970), pp. 340–58.

23 See Barthes' November 1968 article in *Communications*, 'Writing the Event', for his deep reservations about the 'spontaneism' advocated by the May '68 student movement, in *The Rustle of Language*, pp. 149–54.

24 Ibid., p. 105.

25 This was a comment made by Barthes in the televised documentary *Les Archives du xxe siècle*, and edited out of the shortened version of the interview, which was published as 'Réponses', *Tel Quel*, XLIV (Autumn 1971); see 'Responses. Interview with *Tel Quel*', trans. Vérène

Grieshaber, in *The Tel Quel Reader*, ed. Patrick ffrench and Roland-François Lack (London, 1998), pp. 249–67.

26 Bernard Brillant, *Les Clercs de '68* (Paris, 2003), p. 64.

27 In 1977 for example, Barthes was among many intellectuals to sign a petition in favour of the decriminalization of sexual relations between adults and minors; see Julian Bourg, *From Revolution to Ethics: May 1968 and Contemporary French Thought* (Montreal, 2007), p. 205.

28 Jon Whitley, 'Interview with Roland Barthes', *Sunday Times* (2 February 1969), p. 55.

29 See Roland Barthes, *Mythologies* (London, 2009), pp. xvii–xviiii.

30 Barthes, *The Rustle of Language*, pp. 150–51.

31 Barthes, '*Sarrasine' de Balzac*, pp. 315–17. The English title 'To the Seminar', in *The Rustle of Language*, pp. 332–42, loses the ambiguity of the French 'Au séminaire', in which Barthes was playing on a double meaning: the location ('In the Seminar Room') and the dedication 'To the Seminar'.

32 *OC*, III, 102–3. See Ralph Haendels, Abderrahman Gharouia and Ridha Boulaâbi's very different readings of *Incidents*, and my article on Morsy's poem, in Ridha Boulaâbi et al., eds, *Barthes au Maroc* (Meknes, 2013).

33 Barthes, *The Grain of the Voice*, p. 112.

34 Ironically, in his popular theatre days in the 1950s, Barthes had roundly criticized this play in 1959 (*OC*, I, 981–3).

35 Édouard Glissant, 'Le Chaos-monde : Entre l'oral et l'écrit', in *Paroles de Nuit: La nouvelle littérature antillaise*, ed. Ralph Ludwig (Paris, 1994).

36 Roland Barthes, *Empire of Signs*, trans. Richard Howard (London, 1983), pp. 48–57.

37 Gil, *Roland Barthes: Au lieu de la vie*, p. 342; Paul Reboux and Charles Müller were famous for their pastiches in the series *A la manière de . . .* (In the Manner of . . .), published between 1908 and 1914 (when Müller dies), and at exactly the same time as the *En marge de . . .* series by Jules Lemaître that we mentioned in Chapter One; continued by Reboux until 1950, the series was considered a little simplistic and old-fashioned by then.

38 J. Starobinski, *Words upon Words: The Anagrams of Ferdinand de Saussure* [1971], trans. Olivia Emmett (Ann Arbor, MI, 1999); his first article on Saussure's anagrams had appeared in 1964 in the *Mercure de France*, however.

39 É. Marty, 'Roland Barthes et le discours clinique: Lecture de *s/z*', *Essaim*, xv (2005), pp. 83–100; and Gil, *Roland Barthes: Au lieu de la vie*, pp. 92–5.

40 Diana Knight makes interesting connections between money and sex in her reading of Barthes' description, in *Empire of Signs*, of the popular leisure activity in Tokyo, the slot machines called *pachinko*; Barthes' account of the silver liquid that is the money that falls into your hand if you win looks, to Knight, much like an allusion to male masturbation (Knight also roundly rebukes Barthes in *Incidents* for his colonialist exploitation of Moroccan boys); see Diana Knight, Chapters Five and Six in *Barthes and Utopia: Space, Travel, Writing* (Oxford, 1997).

41 Roland Barthes, *s/z*, trans. Richard Miller (London, 1975), p. 21.

42 Barthes, 'Index, Sign, Money', in *s/z*, pp. 39–40. Poverty also emerged from the notion of the 'inorigin' of wealth; in Morocco in 1969, Barthes showed himself acutely aware of how poverty came across in modern society, when he roundly criticized European and North American Hippies in Morocco for 'imitating' the true poverty of destitution. See Roland Barthes, 'A Case of Cultural Criticism', in *The Language of Fashion*, trans. Andy Stafford (Oxford and Sydney, 2006), pp. 110–14.

43 'Dandyism and Fashion', in *The Language of Fashion*, pp. 65–9.

44 Barthes, *s/z*, p. 21; see also 'The Dissolve of Voices', in *s/z*, pp. 41–2.

6 From the *École* to the *Collège*

1 On Barthes' understanding of 'amateur', see the 1975 interview 'Twenty Key Words', in Roland Barthes, *The Grain of the Voice: Interviews, 1962–1980*, trans. Linda Coverdale (New York, 1985), pp. 216–18 and 240, where *désaliéné* is translated as 'de-alienated'.

2 Roland Barthes, *The Responsibility of Forms: Critical Essays on Music, Art and Representation*, trans. Richard Howard (Oxford, 1985), pp. 103–28. Erté's real name was Romain de Tirtof.

3 Cécile Hanania, *Roland Barthes et l'étymologie* (Brussels, 2010), p. 107. Also known as an auto-antonym, the *enantioseme* has a rare but excellent example in French in the word *hôte*, which means, equally, 'host' and 'guest'; an example in English would be 'to cleave',

which means both 'to split apart' and 'to join with' (my thanks to Barry Heselwood for this rare example in English).

4 See Guy de Mallac and Margaret Eberbach, *Barthes* (Paris, 1971) and *Tel Quel*, XLIV (1971).

5 See also Dominique de Roux's 1971 collection of aphorisms, *Immédiatement* (Paris, 1972), from which Barthes asked Christian Bourgois, the publisher, to remove the offending page involving a diary-entry discussion between de Roux and Jean Genet about Barthes' homosexuality.

6 Roland Barthes, 'Rasch', in *The Responsibility of Forms*, pp. 299–312; and Barthes, 'The Grain of the Voice', in ibid., pp. 299–312 and pp. 269–76.

7 Roland Barthes, 'From Work to Text', in *Image-Music-Text*, trans. Stephen Heath (Glasgow, 1977), pp. 155–64.

8 See, for example, the section in Roland Barthes, 'From Gemstones to Jewellery', in *The Language of Fashion,* trans. Andy Stafford (Oxford and Sydney, 2006), pp. 63–4.

9 For this reason, Marie Gil's biography of Barthes aims, or claims, to present his own life as a *vie comme texte* (life as text); see Marie Gil, *Roland Barthes: Au lieu de la vie* (Paris, 2012), p. 353. In a sense, she is right to say that Barthes' life for us is already 'text' (especially if, like most of us, one never 'knew' him), in which case, her (and our) writing of his life cannot but be 'textual' and 'fictional'. In the conclusion, we will briefly consider just how 'parametric' with Barthes' life her biography really is.

10 See the discussion around the term in the 1975 interview 'Twenty Key Words', in *The Grain of the Voice*, pp. 222–4.

11 Roland Barthes, *Oeuvres complètes*, ed. Éric Marty (Paris, 2002), vol. III, p. 705; Roland Barthes, *The Preparation of the Novel: Lecture Courses and Seminars at the Collège de France (1978–1980)*, trans. Kate Briggs (New York, 2011), pp. 207–8; Roland Barthes, *Le Lexique de l'auteur: Séminaire à l'École pratique des hautes études, 1973–1974* (Paris, 2010), p. 68.

12 In the discussion in Cerisy about 'Image', it was proposed that everything Barthes had said about image suggested that the conference was tantamount to a continuation of Montaigne's essays; so Barthes dropped in, humorously, the idea that he had never read Montaigne! It was a pleasure to come to later, he added, and they were both *Gascons*; see A. Compagnon, ed., *Colloque de Cerisy* (Paris, 1978), pp. 321–2.

13 See Barthes, 'Responses. Interview with *Tel Quel*', trans. Vérène Grieshaber, in *The Tel Quel Reader*, ed. Patrick ffrench and Roland-François Lack (London, 1998), p. 260; Roland Barthes, *Roland Barthes by Roland Barthes*, trans. Richard Howard (London, 1977), p. 161.

14 Roland Barthes, *The Rustle of Language*, trans. Richard Howard (Oxford, 1986), p. 79.

15 Barthes even wrote a 'review' of his own biography of the self/of himself – see 'Barthes puissance trois' ('Barthes to the Power of Three'), in *OC*, IV, 775–7. The recently published seminar notes, *Le Lexique de l'auteur*, contain some previously unpublished fragments from *Roland Barthes by Roland Barthes*.

16 Published in English as Roland Barthes, *Travels in China* (Cambridge, 2012).

17 See, for example, ibid., pp. 91–2, 102.

18 Helpfully, this seminar is reproduced in the record of Barthes' seminar experiments with the image of the self, *Le Lexique de l'auteur*, pp. 227–45.

19 The essay was republished a year later in pamphlet form by Christian Bourgois (*OC*, IV, 516–20).

20 See Barthes, 'Alors, la Chine?', *OC*, IV, 518, 519.

21 *OC*, III, 1044; Roland Barthes, *The Neutral: Lecture Course at the Collège de France, 1977–1978*, trans. Rosalind Krauss and Denis Hollier (New York, 2005), pp. 176–7.

22 See Barthes, 'Inaugural Lecture, Collège de France', in *A Barthes Reader*, ed. Susan Sontag (New York, 1982), pp. 457 and 461.

23 Roland Barthes, *The Semiotic Challenge*, trans. Richard Howard (Oxford, 1987), p. 285.

24 Again, like *Le Lexique de l'auteur*, the recently published seminar notes *Le Discours Amoureux: Séminaire à l'École pratique des hautes études, 1974–1976* (Paris, 2007) also contain some fascinating excerpts not included in the final book version, and, again, unfortunately not yet available in English translation.

25 Directed at the Théâtre Marie-Stuart in 1978 by Pierre Leenhardt, *The Lover's Discourse* stage production was discussed by Barthes in an interview (*OC*, V, 545–7).

26 Roland Havas apparently 'inspired' *A Lover's Discourse* just as the 'Olivier crisis' had been the personal motivation behind *On Racine*.

27 Indeed, in this mid-1970s period of alternative forms of living together,

some of Barthes' close friends (though all much younger than he) – Youssef Baccouche, Jean-Louis Bouttes and Paul Le Jéloux – lived together in a homosexual threesome, just one example of an (avant-garde) 'How to live together'.

28 Roland Barthes, *How to Live Together*, trans. Kate Briggs (New York, 2013), p. 131.

29 Ibid., pp. 12–13, 38–41. See Maarten De Pourcq, '"The *Paideia* of the Greeks": On the Methodology of Roland Barthes' *Comment vivre ensemble*', *Paragraph*, XXXI/1 (2008), pp. 23, 26–7, 33.

30 Roland Barthes, *A Lover's Discourse: Fragments*, trans. Richard Howard (London, 1990), pp. 232–4.

31 Barthes, *How to Live Together*, p. 132.

32 Ibid., pp. 21, 133.

33 Ibid., p. 23.

34 All this helped Barthes in *How to Live Together*, p. 131, to muse on the optimal number of people for the idiorrythmy to work; in the Ceylon monastery, it was 'about ten'; for the modern 'parahippy' (that is, American) communities, around 20–30 on average; and in France the number was fifteen; whereas for Barthes' own idiorrythmy, he would prefer eight to ten people as an upper limit. At the same time as these lectures, Barthes quoted Schopenhauer's deeply pessimistic metaphor of the couple as like porcupines – warm for the other porcupine to cuddle up to, but painful due to the spikes; see *Le Discours amoureux*, p. 452.

35 Barthes, *Mythologies*, pp. 93–6.

36 Barthes, *The Neutral*, pp. 32, 175–86.

37 Roland Barthes, *Empire of Signs*, trans. Richard Howard (London, 1983), pp. 19–22.

38 Barthes, *The Neutral*, pp. 34–5.

39 Ibid., p. 36.

40 Ibid., p. 29.

41 Ibid., p. xxv.

42 'The Image' has been translated, in Barthes, *The Rustle of Language*, pp. 350–58, but the discussion afterwards has not.

43 Ibid., pp. 351, 355.

44 Ibid., pp. 56–7; Collective, *Colloque de Cerisy*, pp. 317–18.

45 Barthes, *The Rustle of Language*, p. 357.

46 See Barthes' essay on his hesitations about using the writer's 'journal', 'Deliberation', in *The Rustle of Language*, pp. 359–73.

47 Barthes, *The Grain of the Voice*, p. 330.

7 Fame, Death and the 'Aristocratic' Self

1 All three of these special numbers on Barthes published 'old', recycled material by him; his first published essay on Gide and his *Journal* from 1942 in *Magazine littéraire* – see Susan Sontag, ed., *A Barthes Reader* (New York, 1982), pp. 3–17; his parody of *Criton* from 1933 in *L'Arc* in 1974 – see Roland Barthes, *Oeuvres complètes*, ed. Éric Marty (Paris, 2002), vol. IV, pp. 497–501; and (one could argue that) the interview 'Réponses' in *Tel Quel* (often considered the moment when Barthes, looking backwards over his career for the first time, began to consider himself, the self) was using the 'text' of his former life as a 'text' for 1971.

2 Followed by *Assez décodé!* (Enough Decoding!) by Racine specialist René Pommier (Paris, 1978), no doubt still smarting after the Picard-Barthes joust ten years before; not content, Pommier then published his *Roland Barthes ras le bol!* (Roland Barthes, Had Enough!) (Paris, 1987).

3 *OC*, V, 330–34, 456–8. See Scott Gunther, *The Elastic Closet: Homosexuality in France, 1942–present* (Basingstoke, 2009), p. 63; compared to Michel Foucault, however, Barthes' homosexuality was carefully hidden, no doubt to avoid offending his mother.

4 *OC*, V, 314–16.

5 See Barthes' preface to Renaud Camus' 'gay' novel *Tricks*, in *The Rustle of Language*, trans. Richard Howard (Oxford, 1986), pp. 291–5. Camus has become horribly anti-Semitic in his later career – in the so-called 'Affaire Camus' of 2000 – and, most recently, he advocated a vote for Front National candidate Marine Le Pen.

6 *OC*, V, 625–53.

7 In his journal *La Règle du jeu* in 1991, Bernard-Henri Lévy published extracts from the lecture course that had been recorded on tape by Laurent Dispot, much to the annoyance of the guardians at Les Éditions du seuil of Barthes' unpublished work; these notes were published in *La Règle du jeu*, V (August 1991), pp. 36–60, under the

title that Barthes had thought about using, 'Le Désir de neutre'.

8 Roland Barthes, *The Neutral: Lecture Course at the Collège de France, 1977–1978*, trans. Rosalind Krauss and Denis Hollier (New York, 2005), pp. 130–35.

9 Ibid., pp. 83–4.

10 Roland Barthes, *The Language of Fashion,* trans. Andy Stafford (Oxford and Sydney, 2006), pp. 65–9.

11 Barthes, *The Neutral*, p. 36.

12 Ibid., pp. 34–5.

13 Ibid., p. 36.

14 Given the mature Barthes' writing on topics other than literature, literary theory and semiology, his attention to visual arts is not that surprising: throughout the 1970s he wrote regular pieces on visual art generally – on Cy Twombly, Bernard Réquichot, Saul Steinberg, Arcimboldo, André Masson, Pierre Frilay and even cartoons by Raymond Savignac and posters and letters by Erté, not to mention pieces on Bernard Buffet, Alexander Calder and Dutch seventeenth-century artists in his early career (he was also friends with Andy Warhol in the 1970s); he further wrote on music (Schumann, Schubert, Panzéra, Pierre Boulez and IRCAM), on a range of photographers (Avedon, Daniel Boudinet, Lucien Clergue, Bernard Faucon and Wilhelm von Gloeden) and on film directors (Antonioni, Gérard Blain, Pier Paolo Pasolini and Eisenstein).

15 Roland Barthes, *The Preparation of the Novel: Lecture Courses and Seminars at the Collège de France (1978–1980)*, trans. Kate Briggs (New York, 2011), pp. 212–13.

16 Roland Barthes, *Mourning Diary. October 26, 1977–September 15, 1979*, trans. Richard Howard (London, 2010), p. 36.

17 Marie Gil, *Roland Barthes: Au lieu de la vie* (Paris, 2012), pp. 18–19; in *The Preparation of the Novel*, pp. 207ff., Barthes even called it 'life as work [*oeuvre*]', no longer 'life as text' which had been the key term of the late 1960s and early 1970s in, for example, 'From Work to Text', in *Image-Music-Text*, pp. 155–64.

18 Gil, *Roland Barthes: Au lieu de la vie*, pp. 20–21; in fact, Gil sees these failures in, or as, an oscillation with his undoubted successes.

19 Once again there were failed consultations with Lacan in 1977; is it any wonder then that his relation to psychoanalysis was 'undecided', Lacan's cure being the polar opposite of the 'neutral' (*oc*, IV, 724)?

20 See Barthes, 'Twenty Key Words', in Roland Barthes, *The Grain of the Voice: Interviews, 1962–1980*, trans. Linda Coverdale (New York, 1985), p. 232.

21 Gil, *Roland Barthes: Au lieu de la vie*, pp. 24–5.

22 *The Preparation of the Novel* also contained a final set of seminar notes that interrogated photographic portraits of late nineteenth-century high society in France, including (on p. 456) Jeanne Proust, Marcel Proust's mother, who was photographed in 1904 a year before her death.

23 Lucy O'Meara discusses this opposition of *album* and *Livre* in relation to Barthes' views on the writer's diary; see O'Meara, *Roland Barthes at the Collège de France* (Liverpool, 2012), pp. 182–9.

24 Barthes, *The Preparation of the Novel*, pp. 189–91.

25 Ibid., pp. 143–4.

26 Roland Barthes, *Le Lexique de l'auteur : Séminaire à l'École pratique des hautes études, 1973–1974* (Paris, 2010), p. 274. 'Human knowledge does not follow a straight line, but endlessly approximates a series of circles, a spiral', wrote V. I. Lenin; see his *Collected Works*, vol. xxxviii (New York, 1981), pp. 357–61.

27 Barthes, *The Preparation of the Novel*, pp. 103–4.

28 Roland Barthes, *A Lover's Discourse: Fragments*, trans. Richard Howard (London, 1990), p. 220.

29 Barthes, *The Preparation of the Novel*, p. 5.

30 Ibid., p. 191.

31 It is difficult not to see this phantom photographic image as a premonition of, and inspiration for, Hervé Guibert's essay-novel *L'Image fantôme* (Paris, 1981).

32 R. Stamelman, Chapter Nine in *Lost Beyond Telling: Representations of Death and Absence in Modern French Poetry* (Ithaca, NY, 1990).

33 Barthes, *The Grain of the Voice*, p. 356.

34 Roland Barthes, *Camera Lucida: Reflections on Photography*, trans. Richard Howard (London, 1984), pp. 92–3.

35 The first of these pieces from the 1950s on Vinaver's theatre (*oc*, I, 646–9) was only published in 1979; see also *oc*, I, 666–7, 887–8.

36 Barthes, *Camera Lucida*, p. 14.

37 'The Third Meaning', in *Image-Music-Text*, trans. Stephen Heath (Glasgow, 1977), pp. 52–68, and 'Rhetoric of the Image', ibid., pp. 15–31; on Pic, see *oc*, I, 276–9.

38 Barthes, *Camera Lucida*, p. 71.

39 Barthes, *Le Lexique de l'auteur*, pp. 324–5.

40 In a short fragment from 1929, Bataille linked the *déclassé* to the *Informe*; see his *Oeuvres complètes*, vol. 1 (Paris, 1971), p. 217. A translation of *déclasse* as 'unclassified' is problematic in English, but it is not discountable in the way that 'declassified' certainly is.

41 Roland Barthes, *Roland Barthes by Roland Barthes*, trans. Richard Howard (London, 1977), p. 45.

42 Barthes, *The Rustle of Language*, p. 354.

43 See Roland Barthes, 'Saussure, the Sign, Democracy' [1973], in *The Semiotic Challenge*, trans. Richard Howard (Oxford, 1987), pp. 155–6.

44 Collective, *Colloque de Cerisy* (Paris, 1978), p. 312.

45 That Barthes was knocked down, and his death hastened, by a laundry van has become the stuff of literary folklore, typified recently by the publication of a collection of short stories by Barthes scholar Thomas Clerc called *L'Homme qui tua Roland Barthes, et autres nouvelles* (Paris, 2010).

Conclusion: 'Barthes is Not a Barthesian'

1 Roland Barthes, *Writing Degree Zero*, trans. Annette Lavers and Colin Smith (London, 1967), p. 20; Roland Barthes, *The Grain of the Voice: Interviews, 1962–1980*, trans. Linda Coverdale (New York, 1985), p. 330.

2 Roland Barthes, 'Inaugural Lecture', in *A Barthes Reader*, ed. Susan Sontag (London and New York, 1982), p. 460.

3 Marie Gil, *Roland Barthes: Au lieu de la vie* (Paris, 2012). p. 325.

4 There is a flavour of the dispute between theories of agency on the one hand and post-structuralism on the other in the bitter argument between the journals *Change* and *Tel Quel*. Set up by Jean-Pierre Faye in 1968 as a rival to *Tel Quel* and as a critique of its detached politics, and inspired by Noam Chomsky rather than Saussure, *Change* (as the name implies) insisted that *Tel Quel* was restricting itself to the human creativity that came from rules, whereas *Change* showed that it was 'creativity that changes the rules'.

5 See Jean-Claude Milner, *Le Pas philosophique de Roland Barthes* (Paris, 2003), p. 58 note 7.

Select Bibliography

Recent editions of Barthes' works in French

Complete Works

Oeuvres complètes, ed. Éric Marty (1st edn, Paris, 1993–95, 3 vols; 2nd edn, Paris, 2002, 5 vols)
Barthes: Anthologie de textes, ed. Claude Coste (Paris, 2010)

Posthumous publications, including journal, lecture
and seminar notes, not in the Complete Works

Comment vivre ensemble. Simulation romanesque de quelques espaces quotidiens. Cours et séminaires au Collège de France (1976–1977) (Paris, 2002)
Le Neutre. Cours au Collège de France (1977–1978) (Paris, 2002)
La Préparation du roman I et II. Cours et séminaires au Collège de France (1978–1979 et 1979–1980) (Paris, 2003)
Le Sport et les hommes (Montreal, 2004)
Le Discours amoureux: Séminaire à l'École pratique des hautes études, 1974–1976 (Paris, 2007)
Carnets de voyage en Chine (Paris, 2009)
Journal de deuil (Paris, 2009)
Le Lexique de l'auteur: Séminaire à l'École pratique des hautes études, 1973–1974 (Paris, 2010)
'Sarrasine' de Balzac. Séminaires à l'École pratique des hautes études (1967–1968 et 1968–1969) (Paris, 2011)
Album. Inédits, correspondances et varia, ed. Éric Marty (Paris, 2015)

Barthes' works in English translation

Elements of Semiology, trans. Annette Lavers and Colin Smith (London, 1967)

Writing Degree Zero, trans. Annette Lavers and Colin Smith (London, 1967)

'Seven Photo Models of *Mother Courage*', trans. Hella Freud Bernays, in
    Tulane Drama Review, XII/1 (1967), pp. 44–55

Critical Essays, trans. Richard Howard (Evanston, IL, 1972)

S/Z, trans. Richard Miller (London, 1975)

The Pleasure of the Text, trans. Richard Howard (London, 1976)

Roland Barthes by Roland Barthes, trans. Richard Howard (London, 1977)

Sade, Fourier, Loyola, trans. Richard Miller (London, 1977)

Image-Music-Text, trans. Stephen Heath (Glasgow, 1977)

The Eiffel Tower and Other Mythologies, trans. Richard Howard
    (New York, 1979)

A Barthes Reader, ed. Susan Sontag (London and New York, 1982)

Empire of Signs, trans. Richard Howard (London, 1983)

Camera Lucida: Reflections on Photography, trans. Richard Howard
    (London, 1984)

The Fashion System, trans. Matthew Ward and Richard Howard
    (London, 1985)

The Grain of the Voice: Interviews, 1962–1980, trans. Linda Coverdale (New
    York, 1985)

The Responsibility of Forms: Critical Essays on Music, Art and Representation,
    trans. Richard Howard (Oxford, 1985)

The Rustle of Language, trans. Richard Howard (Oxford, 1986)

Michelet, trans. Richard Howard (Oxford, 1987)

Criticism and Truth, trans. Katrine Pilcher Keuneman (London, 1987)

The Semiotic Challenge, trans. Richard Howard (Oxford, 1987)

Writer Sollers, trans. Philip Thody (London, 1987)

A Lover's Discourse: Fragments, trans. Richard Howard (London, 1990)

New Critical Essays, trans. Richard Howard (Berkeley, CA, 1990)

On Racine, trans. Richard Howard (Berkeley and Los Angeles, CA, 1992)

Incidents, trans. Richard Howard (Berkeley, CA, 1992)

Mythologies, trans. Annette Lavers (London, 1993; new edn, 2009)

'Responses. Interview with *Tel Quel*', trans. Vérène Grieshaber, in *The Tel
    Quel Reader*, ed. Patrick ffrench and Roland-François Lack (London,
    1998), pp. 249–67

The Neutral: Lecture Course at the Collège de France, 1977–1978, trans. Rosalind
    Krauss and Denis Hollier (New York, 2005)
The Language of Fashion, trans. Andy Stafford (Oxford and Sydney, 2006)
What is Sport?, trans. Richard Howard (London and New Haven, CT, 2007)
Mourning Diary: October 26, 1977–September 15, 1979, trans. Richard Howard
    (London, 2010)
*The Preparation of the Novel. Lecture Courses and Seminars at the College de
    France (1978–1979 and 1979–1980)*, trans. Kate Briggs (New York, 2011)
Travels in China, trans. Andrew Brown (Cambridge, 2012)
How to Live Together, trans. Kate Briggs (New York, 2013)

Context

Althusser, Louis, '*Piccolo teatro*: Bertolazzi and Brecht: Notes on a
    Materialist Theatre' [1962], in *For Marx*, trans. Ben Brewster (London,
    1969), pp. 129–51
Bataille, Georges, *Oeuvres complètes* (Paris, 1971)
Bourg, Julian, *From Revolution to Ethics: May 1968 and Contemporary French
    Thought* (Montreal, 2007)
Brillant, Bernard, *Les Clercs de '68* (Paris, 2003)
Consolini, Marco, *Théâtre populaire, 1953–1964: Histoire d'une revue engagée*
    (Paris, 1998)
Debord, Guy, *Society of the Spectacle*, trans. Fredy Perlman and John Supak
    (London, 1977)
Derrida, Jacques, *Of Grammatology*, trans. Gayatri Spivak (Baltimore, MD,
    1977)
——, *Writing and Difference*, trans. Alan Bass (London and Chicago, IL, 1978)
Dosse, François, *History of Structuralism*, 2 vols, trans. Deborah Glassman
    (Minneapolis, MN, 1998)
Eagleton, Terry, and Drew Milne, eds, *Marxist Literary Theory* (Oxford, 1996)
L'Express (3 June 1968; 17–23 June 1968)
Faure, Edgar, *L'Éducation nationale et la participation* (Paris, 1968)
ffrench, Patrick, *The Time of Theory: A History of Tel Quel (1960–1983)*
    (Oxford, 1995)
——, and Roland-François Lack, eds, *The Tel Quel Reader* (London, 1998)
Genette, Gérard, *Bardadrac* (Paris, 2006)

Glissant, Édouard, 'Le Chaos-monde. Entre l'oral et l'écrit', in *Paroles de Nuit: La nouvelle littérature antillaise*, ed. Ralph Ludwig (Paris, 1994)

Godelier, Maurice, 'System, Structure and Contradiction in *Das Kapital*' [1966], trans. Philip Brew, in *Structuralism: A Reader*, ed. M. Lane (London, 1970), pp. 340–58

Groupe d'études théoriques, *Théorie d'ensemble* (Paris, 1968)

Guibert, Hervé, *L'Image fantôme* (Paris, 1981)

Gunther, Scott, *The Elastic Closet: Homosexuality in France, 1942–Present* (Basingstoke, 2009)

Hjelmslev, Louis, *Prolégomènes à une théorie du langage* (Copenhagen, 1943; Paris, 1968)

Lacan, Jacques, *Écrits: A Selection*, trans. Alan Sheridan (London, 1977)

Lévy, Bernard-Henri, 'Le désir de neutre', *La Règle du jeu*, v (August 1991), pp. 36–60

Kristeva, Julia, *The Samourai: A Novel*, trans. Frank Towne (New York, 1992)

Maniglier, Philippe, *La Vie énigmatique des signes. Saussure et la naissance du structuralisme* (Paris, 2006)

Moi, Toril, ed., *The Kristeva Reader* (Oxford, 1986)

Morin, Edgar, 'La fin d'un commencement', in *Arguments 1956–1962*, 2 vols (facs. edn, Toulouse, 1983, ed. Olivier Corpet and Mariateresa Padova), vol. II, pp. 123–6

Nadeau, Maurice, *Grâces leur soient rendues* (Paris, 1990)

New Oxford Companion to Literature in French, ed. Peter France (Oxford, 1995)

Paz, Octavio, *Early Poems, 1935–1955*, trans. Muriel Rukeyser (New York, 1973)

Picard, Raymond, *New Criticism or New Fraud?*, trans. Frank Towne (Washington, DC, 1969)

Posner, Charles, ed., *Reflections on the Revolution in France: 1968* (London, 1970)

Roux, Dominique de, *Immédiatement* (Paris, 1971)

Stamelman, Richard, *Lost Beyond Telling: Representations of Death and Absence in Modern French Poetry* (Ithaca, NY, 1990)

Starobinski, J, *Words upon Words: The Anagrams of Ferdinand de Saussure* [1971], trans. Olivia Emmett (Ann Arbor, MI, 1999)

Books and Journals on Barthes

Allen, Graham, *Roland Barthes* (London, 2003)

Alphant, Marianne and Nathalie Léger, eds, *R/B. Roland Barthes. Catalogue de l'exposition Centre-Pompidou* (Paris, 2002)

L'Arc, LVI (1974)

Badmington, Neil, ed, *Roland Barthes: Critical Evaluations in Cultural Theory*, 4 vols (London and New York, 2010)

Bensmaïa, Réda, *The Barthes Effect: The Essay as Reflective Text* (Minneapolis, MN, 1987)

Boulaâbi, Ridha, Claude Coste and Mohamed Lehdahda, eds, *Barthes au Maroc* (Meknes, 2013)

Brown, Andrew, *Roland Barthes: The Figures of Writing* (Oxford, 1992)

Burnier, Michel-Antoine and Patrick Rambaud, *Le Roland-Barthes sans peine* (Paris, 1978)

Calvet, Louis-Jean, *Roland Barthes: 1915–1980* (Paris, 1990), trans. Sarah Wykes (Oxford and Cambridge, 1994)

Cartier, J.-C., 'Roland Barthes' Resurrection of the Author and Redemption of Biography', *Cambridge Quarterly*, XXIX/4 (2000), pp. 386–93

Clerc, Thomas, *L'Homme qui tua Roland Barthes, et autres nouvelles* (Paris, 2010)

Comment, Bernard, *Roland Barthes: Vers le neutre* (Paris, 1991)

Compagnon, Antoine, ed., *Prétexte: Roland Barthes/Colloque de Cerisy* (Paris, 1978)

Coquio, Catherine, and Régis Salado, eds, *Barthes après Barthes: une actualité en questions* (Pau, 1993)

Coste, Claude, *Roland Barthes, moraliste* (Lille, 1998)

——, *Bêtise de Barthes* (Paris, 2011)

Culler, Jonathan, *Barthes: A Very Short Introduction* (2nd edn, Oxford, 2002)

Europe, 952–3 (September 2008)

Freedman, Sanford, and Carole Anne Taylor, eds, *Roland Barthes: A Bibliographical Readers' Guide* (New York and London, 1983)

Gane, Mike and Nicholas, *Roland Barthes*, 3 vols (London, 2004)

Genesis: Manuscrits, recherche, invention, 19 (2002), special number on 'Roland Barthes'

Gil, Marie, *Roland Barthes: Au lieu de la vie* (Paris, 2012)

Green, A., 'Les *Mythologies* de Roland Barthes et la psychopathologie', *Critique*, CXXXII (1958), pp. 105–13

Hanania, Cécile, *Roland Barthes et l'étymologie* (Brussels, 2010)

Heath, Stephen, *Vertige du Déplacement: Lecture de Barthes* (Paris, 1974)

Jeannelle, J.-L, 'Barthes ne se laisse pas faire', *Le Monde des livres* (9 March 2012)

Kelly, Michael, 'Demystification: A Dialogue Between Barthes and Lefebvre', *Yale French Studies*, XCVIII (2000), pp. 79–94

Knight, Diana, *Barthes and Utopia: Space, Travel, Writing* (Oxford, 1997)

——, ed., *Critical Essays on Roland Barthes* (New York, 2000)

Lavers, Annette, *Roland Barthes: Structuralism and After* (London and Boston, MA, 1982)

Lombardo, Patrizia, *The Three Paradoxes of Roland Barthes* (Athens, GA, 1989)

Le Magazine littéraire (February 1975; October 1993; January 2009; May 2013)

Mallac, Guy de and Margaret Eberbach, *Barthes* (Paris, 1971)

Maniglier, Philippe, *La Vie énigmatique des signes. Saussure et la naissance du structuralisme* (Paris, 2006)

Marty, Éric, *Le Métier d'écrire* (Paris, 2006)

——, 'Roland Barthes et le discours clinique: Lecture de *s/z*', in *Essaim*, XV (2005), pp. 83–100

Miller, D. A., *Bringing Out Roland Barthes* (Berkeley and Los Angeles, CA, 1992)

Milner, Jean-Claude, *Le Pas philosophique de Roland Barthes* (Paris, 2003)

Moriarty, Michael, *Roland Barthes* (Cambridge and Oxford, 1991)

Nottingham French Studies, XXXVI/1 (Spring 1997); XLVII/2 (Summer 2008)

O'Meara, Lucy, *Roland Barthes at the Collège de France* (Liverpool, 2012)

Paragraph, XI (1988); XXXI/1 (2008)

Pint, Kris, *The Perverse Art of Reading: On the Phantasmatic Semiology in Roland Barthes' Cours au Collège de France* (Amsterdam, 2010)

Poétique, XLVII (September 1981)

Pommier, René, *Assez décodé!* (Paris, 1978)

——, *Roland Barthes ras le bol!* (Paris, 1987)

De Pourcq, Maarten, '"The *Paideia* of the Greeks": On the Methodology of Roland Barthes' *Comment vivre ensemble*', *Paragraph*, XXXI/1 (2008), pp. 23–37

Rabaté, Jean-Michel, ed., *Writing the Image after Roland Barthes* (Philadelphia, PA, 1997)

Robbe-Grillet, Alain, *Why I Love Barthes*, trans. Andrew Brown (Cambridge, 2011)

Roger, Philippe, *Roland Barthes: roman* (Paris, 1986)

Samoyault, Tiphaine, *Roland Barthes* (Paris, 2015)

Sontag, Susan, ed., *A Barthes Reader* (New York, 1982)

Stafford, Andy, *Roland Barthes, Phenomenon and Myth: An Intellectual Biography* (Edinburgh, 1998)

Tel Quel, XLVII (1971)

Thody, Philip, *Roland Barthes: A Conservative Estimate* (London, 1977)

Ungar, Steven, *Roland Barthes: The Professor of Desire* (London and Lincoln, NE, 1983)

White, Ed, *How to Read Barthes' Image-Music-Text* (London, 2012)

Whitley, Jon, 'Interview with Roland Barthes', *Sunday Times* (2 February 1969), p. 55.

Wiseman, Mary Bittner, *The Ecstasies of Roland Barthes* (London, 1989)

CDs of Barthes' lectures

Comment vivre ensemble (Seuil, 2003)

Le Neutre (Seuil, 2003)

La Préparation du roman (Seuil, 2003)

Online

www.roland-barthes.org

http://sites.cardiff.ac.uk/barthes

Acknowledgements

I am grateful to the University of Leeds for research leave, and to the Arts Faculty for financial help with illustrations; also to Neil Badmington, Ridha Boulaâbi, Claude Coste, Charles Forsdick, Martin Hamblen, Richard Hibbitt, Richard Howard, Roxane Jubert, Claire Lozier, Robin Mackenzie, Éric Marty, Zaghloul Morsy, Laure Papin, Claudia Amigo Pino, Nigel Saint and Caroline Stride. My thanks go as well to colleagues at the University of Kent (especially Katja Haustein, Tom Baldwin and Lucy O'Meara) for inviting me to give a paper at the 'What's So Great about Roland Barthes?' seminar series in November 2013, and which led to this book. I am particularly indebted to Barry Heselwood who kindly read a first draft, to Diana Knight who made very helpful comments on a later draft, to the anonymous reader and to Vivian Constantinopoulos and Amy Salter at Reaktion Books.

Photo Acknowledgements

The author and the publishers wish to express their thanks to the below sources of illustrative material and /or permission to reproduce it.

Arnaud 25: p. 80; Corbis: pp. 34, 115, 131, 133 (Sophie Bassouls/Sygma), 154 (Jacques Pavlovsky/Sygma); Getty Images: pp. 85 (AFP), 112 (photo by Louis MONIER/Gamma-Rapho via Getty Images), 140 (photo by Ulf Andersen), 152 (photo by Gilbert UZAN/Gamma-Rapho via Getty Images); REX Shutterstock: pp. 14 (Sipa Press), 103 (Denis Cameron); © RMN-Grand Palais – Gestion droit d'auteur, Localisation: Charenton-le-Pont, Médiathèque de l'Architecture et du Patrimoine, Photo © Ministère de la Culture – Médiathèque du Patrimoine, Dist. RMN-Grand Palais/Daniel Boudinet: p. 104; © Caroline Stride: p. 156.